Holiday Story Play
Costumes, Cooking, Music, and More
PreK-4

Joyce Harlow

Victoria Saibara

1993
TEACHER IDEAS PRESS
A Division of
Libraries Unlimited, Inc.
Englewood, Colorado

TEACHER IDEAS PRESS
A Division of
Libraries Unlimited, Inc.
P.O. Box 6633
Englewood, Colorado 80155-6633

Library of Congress Cataloging-in-Publication Data

Harlow, Joyce.
　　Holiday story play : costumes, cooking, music, and more, preK-4 /
Joyce Harlow, Victoria Saibara.
　　xvii, 199 p.　22x28 cm.
　　Includes bibliographical references.
　　ISBN 1-56308-115-6
　　1. Holidays--Study and teaching (Elementary)　2. Drama in
education.　I. Saibara, Victoria.　II. Title.
GT3933.H38　1993
371.3'32--dc20　　　　　　　　　　　　　　　　　　93-24792
　　　　　　　　　　　　　　　　　　　　　　　　　　　　CIP

Holiday Story Play

To my granddaughter,
Kathryn Joyce,
my daughters,
Victoria and Pamela,
and
to all of my students who have
accompanied me on the
joyful journey of discovery.

Joyce Harlow

To my kindergarten students
at Galatas Elementary
in The Woodlands, Texas.

Victoria Saibara

CONTENTS

INTRODUCTION

Each holiday theme in *Holiday Story Play* is designed to integrate literature with dramatic play, reading, writing, art, cooking, math, science, music, and cooperative group experiences. Each experience is designed to be child-initiated and developmentally appropriate for any age level. The book can be used either as a whole curriculum or in parts to complement an existing program. Each thematic unit can last from two to three weeks, depending upon the teacher and the students. The teacher sets the stage and then becomes the facilitator of the learning process. The stage is set with the introduction of the holiday theme through the literature. The costumes, masks, play props, and puppets start the process of experiencing.

The "Drama/Play Experience" is introduced through simpletees costumes made in advance by the teacher. The face masks and stick puppets can be made by the teacher or by the children. The patterns provided here are designed with minimal illustrated features to allow the children more freedom for their own interpretation of the characters.

The "Literature/Writing Experience" uses books about various holidays. After experiencing the stories and the drama play, the children write their own stories. This is a group activity with the children dictating the story to the teacher. The story is written on a large sheet of chart paper. The teacher can play word games with the story by asking if anyone can find a word that they know. The children then play with the story and read it themselves or read it to their friends. The teacher may provide a small pointer for them to use.

The key-word books are prepared in advance by the teacher. Each book measures 3 inches by 6 inches with approximately five sheets of paper between the covers. The sheets of paper inside are unlined to allow for the development of fine motor skills. The key words are written on word cards and placed in a writing center for an independent activity. The teacher introduces the words by writing and verbalizing each word as he or she places them in a basket or pocket chart. The children repeat the word and then play word games with the teacher and other children. The children can play the word game with each other as an open-ended activity. The key words can also be used with the shape book developed for each theme. The shape book allows the children to become authors and illustrators of their own stories. The cover can be traced from a template by the children; the inner white pages are precut by the teacher. The books are stapled together with as many pages as the teacher feels is appropriate for the students. The key words allow the children to choose the writing to go with their illustrations and are completely open-ended to accommodate individual differences and desires.

The "Cooperative/Group Experience" designed for each holiday theme fosters social acceptance, interaction, and problem solving as a whole. Parents are often involved in this process by contributing the needed props or food.

The "Art/Writing Experience" always includes a tempera or watercolor painting to go with the holiday theme. The paintings lend themselves to written captions and can be bound together for a classroom book to be placed in the book center.

"Cooking/Math Experience" is combined to naturally introduce beginning math concepts and skills. Each holiday theme uses a simple recipe for an independent cooking activity with very little teacher interaction.

The "Science/Discovery Experience" includes scientific facts wherever they can be brought in. A discovery museum of contributions and collections related to each holiday theme provides opportunities for exploration.

The "Music/Game Experience" includes original music to go with each holiday theme. With Pamela Copus's help, we designed musical experiences that set *Holiday Story Play* apart and provide the unifying element for the whole concept of the experiences. *Holiday Story Play Music* is teacher-friendly and easy to use with the book or as a separate music experience.

The name *simpletees* describes the basic concept of the costumes designed for each holiday theme. The base of all the costumes is an extra-large short-sleeved T-shirt. These are the easiest for the children to pull over their clothing. Felt and fake fur are used with the T-shirts because they require no finished edges. A hot glue gun is used to attach all the pieces to the costume. A cardboard should be slipped inside the T-shirt to prevent it from sticking together while gluing. A craft stick can be used to press the fabric into the hot glue. Because of the glue gun's high temperatures, costumes should not be made in the presence of children. Because each thematic unit is designed to last only two to three weeks, the costumes receive minimal wear and tear, and thus can be reused for several years. Hang the costumes when not in use to allow wrinkles to fall out. The simpletees are fun to make and can be shared with other teachers.

CHAPTER 1

JOHNNY APPLESEED

DRAMA/PLAY EXPERIENCE

Read *Johnny Appleseed* by Reeve Lindbergh to introduce the theme of Johnny Appleseed. (See bibliography on page 15.) This lyrical and beautifully illustrated tale tells how John Chapman became the legendary distributor of apple seeds and trees across the Midwest. John Chapman's birthday is celebrated on 26 September. Demonstrate the simpletees costumes and play props.

Simpletees Costumes

Use the simpletees costumes of Johnny Appleseed and Hannah Goodwin for a dramatic play experience. (See figure 1.1.) These costumes are based on Reeve Lindbergh's version of *Johnny Appleseed.*

Play Props

Play props can include plastic apples, white or pink plastic apple blossoms, a straw apple basket, a cloth or burlap sack, and a tin sauce pan to use for dramatizing the story of Johnny Appleseed.

Face Masks

Create face masks of Johnny Appleseed and Hannah Goodwin. Use tagboard templates and trace the patterns. Illustrate the masks with facial features for the various characters. (See figures 1.2 and 1.3.)

Stick Puppets/Paper Bag Theater

Make stick puppets of Johnny Appleseed and Hannah Goodwin. (See figure 1.4.) Create a paper bag theater for the stick puppets and present the story of Johnny Appleseed to a friend or parents. (See figure 1.5.)

(Text continues on page 7.)

Fig. 1.1. Simpletees costumes: Johnny Appleseed.

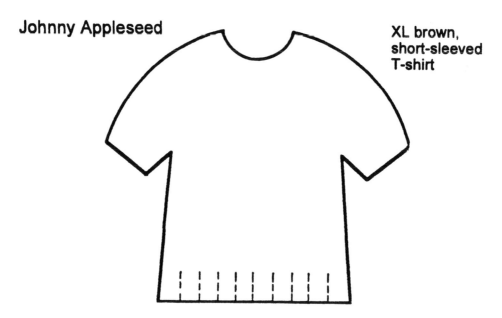

Cut 1 1/2" long X 1" wide fringe along bottom of T-shirt

Glue gun 1 1/4 yd. lace ruffle to bottom of T-shirt

Fig. 1.2. Johnny Appleseed face mask pattern.

Fig. 1.3. Hannah Goodwin face mask pattern.

Fig. 1.4. Johnny Appleseed stick puppet patterns.

Johnny

Hannah

Fig. 1.5. Paper bag puppet theater.

Materials:

What to Do:

Small paper bag
Markers
Scissors
Stapler

Push out sides of bag and flatten.

Cut opening through front and back of bag.

Fold excess length of bag inside.

Staple inside to strengthen sides.

Decorate with markers.

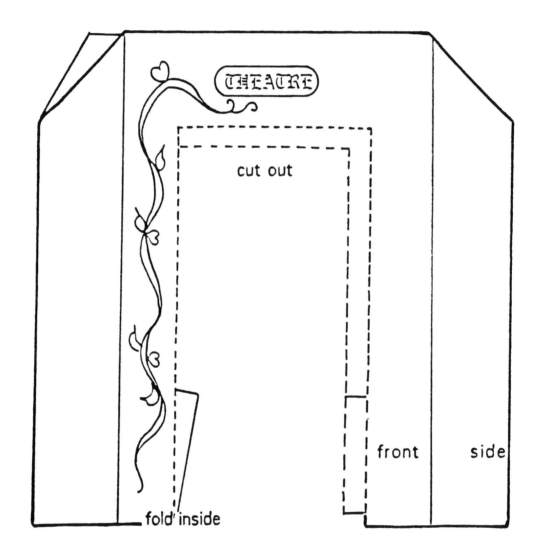

LITERATURE/WRITING EXPERIENCE

Johnny Appleseed *Versions*

Read different versions of "Johnny Appleseed." Steven Kellogg's version gives a vivid account of Johnny Appleseed's legendary feats. Aliki's version emphasizes Johnny's friendship with the native people, pioneers, and wild animals. The seasons and life cycle of the apple are beautifully illustrated in Reeve Lindbergh's poetic version. Compare these versions to Mary Pope Osborne's "Johnny Appleseed" in her anthology *American Tall Tales*. (See bibliography on page 15.)

Johnny Appleseed *Children's Version*

After experiencing the different stories about Johnny Appleseed, write a children's version on a large sheet of chart paper.

Key-Word Books and Key Words

Make a key-word book with the unique or important words from the tale of Johnny Appleseed. The key words for Johnny Appleseed are as follows:

Johnny	Appleseed	Hannah
apple	trees	seed
sack	orchard	plant
sow		

Apple Shape Book

Make an apple shape book by tracing the apple shape from a tagboard template. (See figure 1.6.) Illustrate and write a story about Johnny Appleseed or dictate it to the teacher. Use the key words for an independent writing experience.

Tall Tales

John Chapman was a historical figure whose adventures became legends. Compare and contrast Steven Kellogg's *Johnny Appleseed* with his *Pecos Bill* and *Paul Bunyan*. (See bibliography on page 15.) Tell or write a tall tale about someone in your community.

Fig. 1.6. Apple shape book directions and pattern.

Materials:

Red construction paper
Tagboard
White paper
Scissors
Stapler
Markers or pencils
Key words

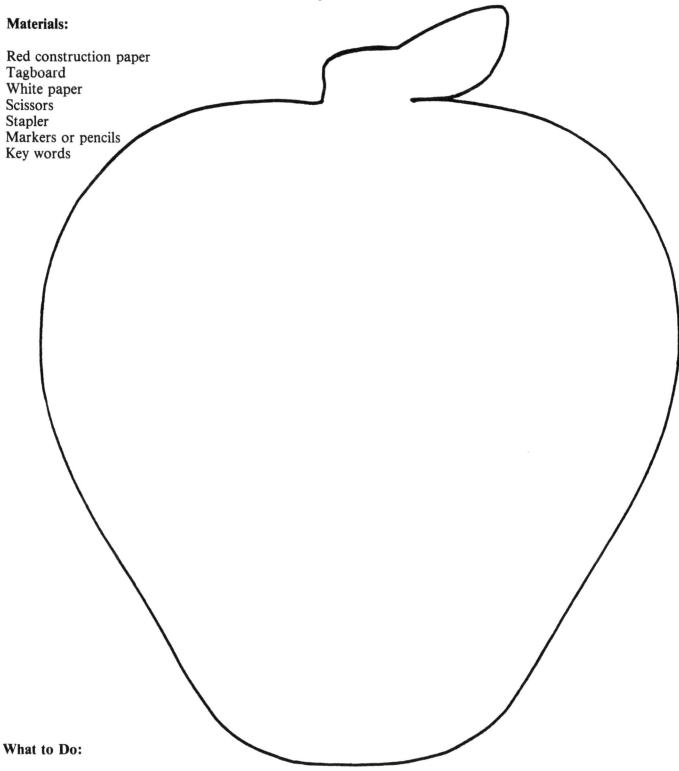

What to Do:

Make a tagboard template from the pattern.

Trace and cut out 2 apple shapes from the construction paper.

Teacher may precut white pages.

Staple the cover and white pages together.

Illustrate the book and write or dictate the story.

Use key words for an independent writing experience.

COOPERATIVE/GROUP EXPERIENCE

Apple Orchard Mural

Discuss the apple orchard mural from Kathy Jakobsen's illustration in *Johnny Appleseed* by Reeve Lindbergh. (See bibliography on page 15.) Work in small groups and paint a mural of an apple orchard. Place a long sheet of mural paper on a table or attach the paper to a wall. Use pink and white tempera for the apple blossoms. Include brown, blue, green, yellow, and red tempera for additional details.

Apple Time Line

In *The Life and Times of the Apple* by Charles Micucci, an enormous collection of facts about apples is presented in an informative and entertaining format. (See bibliography on page 15.) Create an apple time line starting from 2,500,000 B.C. to the 1600s. Working in small groups, write and illustrate a period of time in the life of the apple. Display the different illustrations in sequential order on a wall or bulletin board. Illustrations and stories can also be bound for a classroom book.

ART/CRAFT EXPERIENCE

Tempera Painting

Paint a tempera picture of Johnny Appleseed and Hannah Goodwin. Write or dictate a sentence or story about the picture. Display the paintings on the walls or the bulletin board. Bind the paintings together to make a class book.

Four Seasons Apple Trees

Read *The Seasons of Arnold's Apple Tree* by Gail Gibbons. (See bibliography on page 15.) Arnold's various activities throughout the seasons take place around his favorite apple tree. Illustrate the four seasons of Arnold's apple tree by cutting an 18-by-24-inch piece of construction paper in half to make a 9-by-24-inch long sheet of paper. Fold the paper in fourths. Use crayons or markers and draw a tree trunk on each section. Use pink or white tempera and cotton swabs to paint blossoms on the spring tree. Use red tempera and a cork to stamp apples on the summer tree. Use red tempera and a cork to paint apples on the ground under the fall tree. Leave the winter tree bare.

Stand-Up Apple Trees

My Apple Tree by Harriet Ziefert is another story about the seasons of an apple tree and the joy of eating a fresh-picked apple. (See bibliography on page 15.) Create stand-up apple trees by painting toilet paper tubes and paper plates. (See figure 1.7.)

Apple Printing

Read *Apple Bird* by Brian Wildsmith. (See bibliography on page 15.) Create an illustration for the story by printing with apples. Cut three apples in half. Dip the apple halves into a tray of red, yellow, or green tempera paint. Press the apple prints on a sheet of 12-by-18-inch paper.

Fig. 1.7. Stand-up apple tree directions.

Materials:

Toilet tissue tube
Brown tempera
Green tempera
Red tempera
Corks
Styrofoam tray
Scissors

What to Do:

Paint tissue tube with brown tempera.

Paint small paper plate with green tempera.

Spread a thin layer of red tempera in a Styrofoam tray.

Place cork end in the red tempera and print red apples on the green paper plate.

Cut two slits in one end of tissue tube and insert the green plate for a stand-up apple tree.

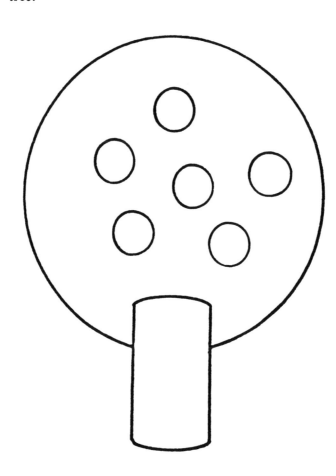

Apple Head Carving

Use a cutting board and a peeler to remove the peel from a large apple. Leave some of the peel on top for hair. Use a plastic knife to carve away parts of the apple to create a nose and a mouth. Use a pencil point to poke in eyes and kernels of popcorn for teeth. Place the apple head in a sunny spot to dry. Check its daily progress and note the changes that occur.

COOKING/MATH EXPERIENCE

Apples to Applesauce

Rain Makes Applesauce by Julian Scheer is a book of delightfully silly passages followed by the refrain "and rain makes applesauce." (See bibliography on page 15.) Making applesauce is a wonderful follow-up to this story. Wash, peel, and cut up two to three pounds of cooking apples. Place the apples in a cooking pot and add ⅓ to ½ cup water. Gently simmer the apples until tender. Remove the pot from heat and allow it to cool somewhat. Mash apples with a potato masher. Sprinkle and stir in ground cinnamon spice. Serve the applesauce while warm in small paper cups.

Charoses

Charoses is a special treat served during the Jewish Passover. Make your own charoses by following the recipe in figure 1.8.

Walking Apple Sandwich

Core an apple and fill it with peanut butter. Take the apple sandwich on a nature walk.

Spicy Cider

Discuss pages 20 and 21 of *The Life and Times of the Apple* by Charles Micucci. (See bibliography on page 15.) Discuss the many uses of the apple that are illustrated in the book. Prepare spicy cider by combining one gallon of apple cider and one cup of brown sugar in a cooking pot. Place two teaspoons of whole cloves and two cinnamon sticks in a cheesecloth bag. Place the bag in the cider and bring to a boil. Simmer for 20 minutes and remove from the heat to cool. Serve warm spicy cider in small paper cups.

Apple Rebus

Read *Who Stole the Apples?* by Sigrid Heuck. (See bibliography on page 15.) Help the animals find out who stole the apples. Solve the rebus and make up your own apple rebus. Make an individual or small group rebus. Be sure to count the number of apples.

Fig. 1.8. Charoses.

Mix together:

½ cup
chopped walnuts

2 cups
chopped apple

½ cup
grape juice

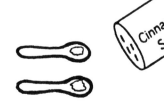

2 teaspoons cinnamon

Apple Party

Celebrate the apple by tasting a variety of apple products. Apples, applesauce, apple butter, dried apples, apple juice or cider, and apple pie can be included in the tasting party. Make a graph to determine which apple products are liked best.

SCIENCE/DISCOVERY EXPERIENCE

Discovery Museum

Create a discovery museum to display and explore items and books related to apples. Have the children contribute a variety of apples and apple products, seeds, books, and other items to the collection. Display the items on a table, shelf, or counter top in the classroom. Use sentence strips to label the items. Explore the museum as a group or individually and look at the ordinary apple in a new way.

Apples to Apples

Fruit: A First Discovery Book by Gallimard Jeunesse and Pascale de Bourgoing explores the apple inside and out. (See bibliography on page 15.) Purchase a variety of apples, such as MacIntosh, Granny Smith, Red Delicious, Golden Delicious, and Winesap. Examine and discuss the similarities and differences of the apples. Wash and slice the different kinds of apples. Remove and examine the seeds with a magnifying glass. Have an apple tasting and make a graph to determine which apples are liked best.

Apple Forest

Examine the photographs of real apple trees in *An Apple Tree Through the Year* by Claudia Schnieper. (See bibliography on page 15.) Cut thin sponges into apple shapes. Place sponge apple shapes on a flat tray. Sprinkle the sponges with rye seed. Use a baster and squirt water on the seeds. Place the seeds in a sunny window and keep the sponges wet. The seeds will sprout an "apple forest" in a few days.

Dried Apples on a String

Use an apple corer and remove the core from a variety of apples. Thread a string through the apples and hang them outside in the sun to dry. Observe the transformation of the apples on a daily basis. Write the daily observations on a sheet of chart paper.

Lupine Lady

Read *Miss Rumphius* by Barbara Cooney. (See bibliography on page 15.) Miss Rumphius wanted to make the world a more beautiful place, so she planted lupine seeds along highways, country roads, fields, and hillsides. Compare and contrast the tale of Johnny Appleseed with *Miss Rumphius*. Order lupine seeds from a seed catalog and plant them inside or outside.

From *Holiday Story Play*, copyright 1993. Libraries Unlimited/Teacher Ideas Press, P.O. Box 6633, Englewood, CO 80155-6633.

MUSIC/GAME EXPERIENCE

Choral Reading

Read *Rain Makes Applesauce* by Julian Scheer. (See bibliography on page 15.) Read a second time and pause for the children to respond "and rain makes applesauce."

Apple Bobbing

Fill a small tub or dishpan with water. Place apples in the water. Children may "bob" for the apples.

Balancing Apples

In *The Legend of William Tell* by Terry Small, the legendary Swiss marksman must shoot an apple off the top of his son's head. (See bibliography on page 15.) By doing so, he changes the course of history. Practice balancing an apple on your head while standing very still. Make it harder by trying to walk while balancing an apple.

Apple Pickin'

Experience the fun of picking apples by singing the song "Apple Pickin'" from *Holiday Story Play Music* by Pamela Copus and Joyce Harlow. (See bibliography on page 15.)

Apple Pickin'

I've been pickin', pickin',
I've been pickin',
Apples all the day long.

Apples in the mornin',
Apples in the evenin',
Apples all the day long.

I've been cookin', cookin',
I've been cookin',
Apples all the day long.

Apples in the dumplin',
Apples in the cider,
Apples all the day long.

I've been dreamin', dreamin',
I've been dreamin',
Apples all the night long.

Apples in the mornin',
Apples in the evenin',
Apples all the day long.

Joyce Harlow

BIBLIOGRAPHY

Aliki. *The Story of Johnny Appleseed*. New York: Prentice-Hall Books for Young Readers, 1963.

Cooney, Barbara. *Miss Rumphius*. New York: Puffin Books, 1982.

Gibbons, Gail. *The Seasons of Arnold's Apple Tree*. New York: Harcourt Brace Jovanovich, 1984.

Heuck, Sigrid. *Who Stole the Apples?* New York: Knopf, 1986.

Jeunesse, Gallimard, and Pascale de Bourgoing. *Fruit: A First Discovery Book*. New York: Scholastic, 1989.

Kellogg, Steven. *Johnny Appleseed*. New York: William Morrow, 1988.

_____. *Paul Bunyan*. New York: William Morrow, 1984.

_____. *Pecos Bill*. New York: William Morrow, 1986.

Lindbergh, Reeve. *Johnny Appleseed*. Boston: Little, Brown, 1990.

Micucci, Charles. *The Life and Times of the Apple*. New York: Orchard Books, 1992.

Osborne, Mary Pope. "Johnny Appleseed," in *American Tall Tales*. New York: Alfred A. Knopf, 1991.

Scheer, Julian. *Rain Makes Applesauce*. New York: Holiday House, 1964.

Schnieper, Claudia. *An Apple Tree Through the Year*. Photographs by Othmar Baumli. Minneapolis, MN: Carolrhoda Books, 1987.

Small, Terry. *The Legend of William Tell*. New York: Bantam Books, 1991.

Wildsmith, Brian. *Apple Bird*. Oxford: Oxford University Press, 1983.

Ziefert, Harriet. *My Apple Tree*. New York: Harper Collins, 1991.

Music

Copus, Pamela, and Joyce Harlow. "Apple Pickin'." *Holiday Story Play Music*. Plano, TX: Dreamtime Productions, P.O. Box 940061, Plano, TX 75094-0061.

COLUMBUS DAY

DRAMA/PLAY EXPERIENCE

Read *In 1492* by Jean Marzollo to introduce the theme of Christopher Columbus and colonization. (See bibliography on page 35.) Written in verse, this book describes Columbus's voyages and his finding of the "New World." Demonstrate the simpletees costumes and play props.

Simpletees Costumes

Use the simpletees costumes of Columbus, King Ferdinand, Queen Isabella, and a Native American for a dramatic play experience. (See figures 2.1 and 2.2.)

Play Props

Play props can include a treasure chest with trinkets; compass; telescope; hourglass; rope; banner; plastic foods, such as ears of corn, potatoes, peppers, and pineapples; and stuffed cats.

Face Masks

Create face masks of Columbus, King Ferdinand, Queen Isabella, and a Native American. Use tagboard templates and trace the different characters. (See figures 2.3, 2.4, 2.5, and 2.6.)

Stick Puppets/Paper Bag Theater

Make stick puppets of Columbus, King Ferdinand, Queen Isabella, and a Native American. (See figure 2.7.) Create a paper bag theater for the stick puppets. (See figure 1.5 on page 6.) Present the story of Christopher Columbus and his adventures to a friend or take home and present to parents.

(Text continues on page 24.)

Fig. 2.1. Simplestees costumes: Columbus Day.

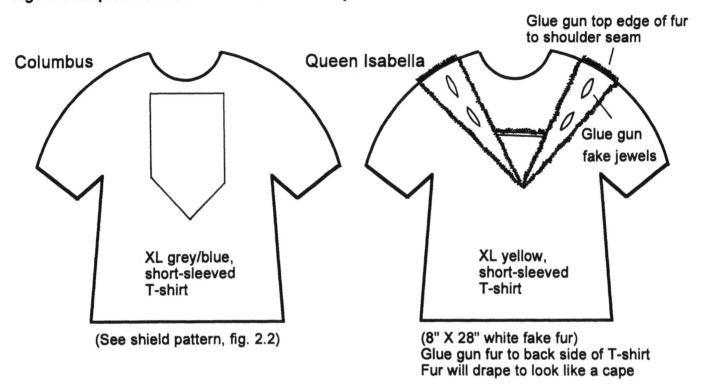

Columbus

XL grey/blue,
short-sleeved
T-shirt

(See shield pattern, fig. 2.2)

Queen Isabella

Glue gun top edge of fur
to shoulder seam

Glue gun
fake jewels

XL yellow,
short-sleeved
T-shirt

(8" X 28" white fake fur)
Glue gun fur to back side of T-shirt
Fur will drape to look like a cape

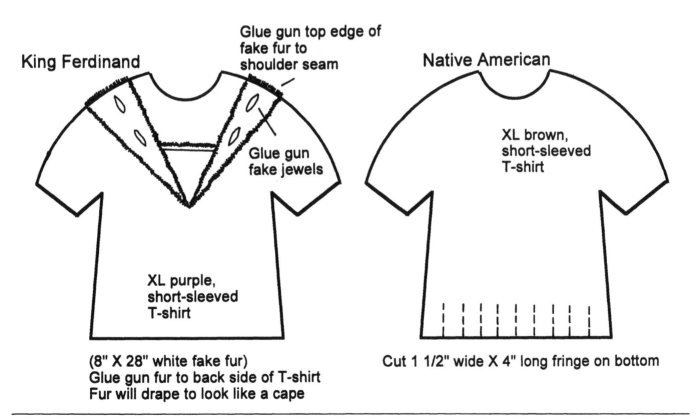

King Ferdinand

Glue gun top edge of
fake fur to
shoulder seam

Glue gun
fake jewels

XL purple,
short-sleeved
T-shirt

(8" X 28" white fake fur)
Glue gun fur to back side of T-shirt
Fur will drape to look like a cape

Native American

XL brown,
short-sleeved
T-shirt

Cut 1 1/2" wide X 4" long fringe on bottom

Fig. 2.2. Columbus shield pattern.

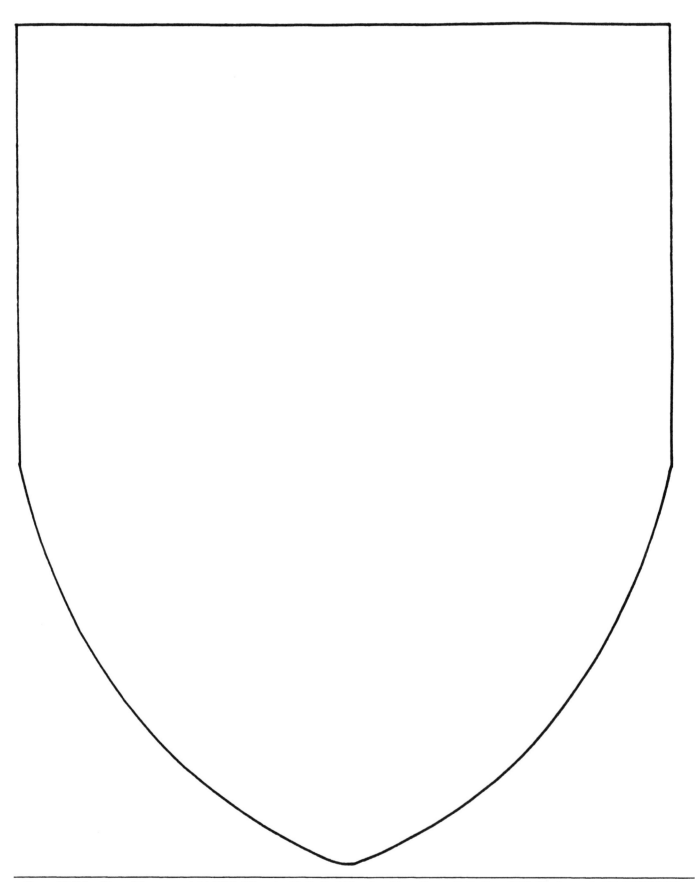

Fig. 2.3. Columbus face mask pattern.

Fig. 2.4. King Ferdinand face mask pattern.

Fig. 2.5. Queen Isabella face mask pattern.

From *Holiday Story Play*, copyright 1993. Libraries Unlimited/Teacher Ideas Press, P.O. Box 6633, Englewood, CO 80155-6633.

Fig. 2.6. Native American face mask pattern.

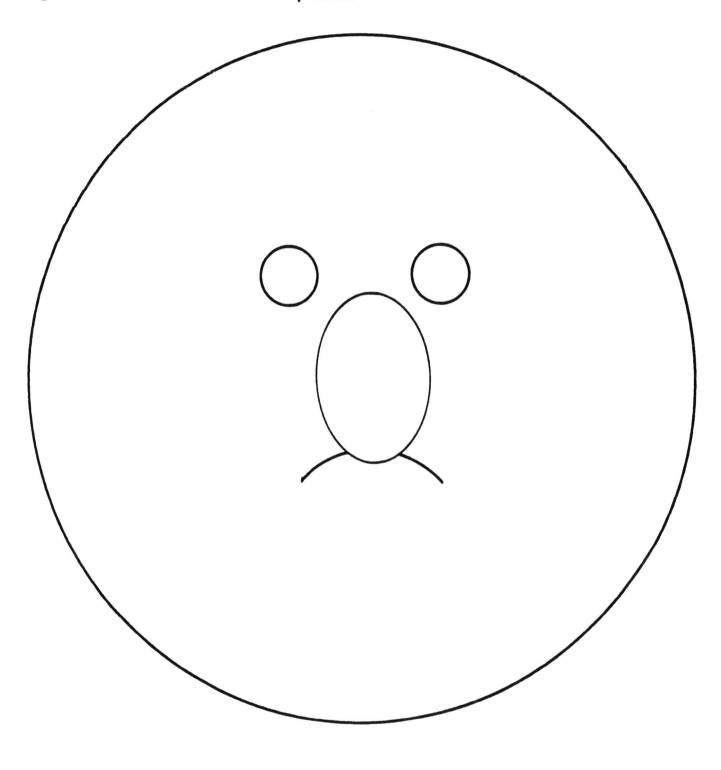

Fig. 2.7. Columbus Day stick puppet patterns.

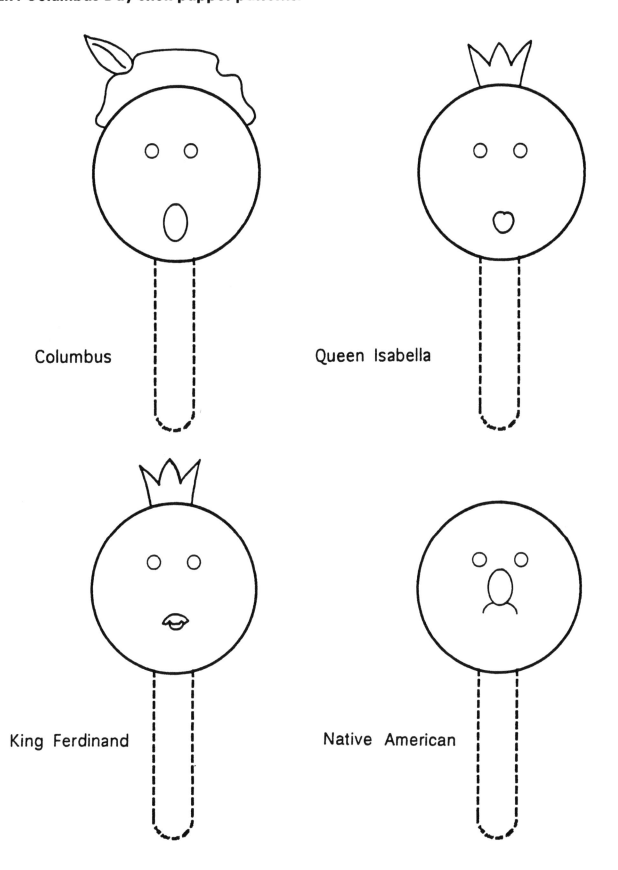

Columbus

Queen Isabella

King Ferdinand

Native American

LITERATURE/WRITING EXPERIENCE

Christopher Columbus *Versions*

Experience a variety of books about Christopher Columbus. For example, *The Voyages of Columbus* by Ken Hills offers a wealth of information on many aspects of Columbus's travels. Carol Greene's *Christopher Columbus: A Great Explorer* uses illustrations from various collections and archives. *The Great Adventure of Christopher Columbus* by Jean Fritz is beautifully illustrated with three-dimensional scenes by Tomie dePaola. Jane Yolen's *Encounter* is the story of Columbus as seen through the eyes of a Taino boy. (See bibliography on page 34.)

Christopher Columbus *Children's Version*

Write a children's version about Christopher Columbus on a large sheet of chart paper.

Key-Word Books and Key Words

Make a key-word book with the unique or important words from the story of Christopher Columbus. The key words for Christopher Columbus are as follows:

Columbus	Niña	Pinta
Santa Maria	compass	sail
ocean	Spain	navigator
Native American		

Ship Shape Book

Make a ship shape book by tracing the ship shape from a tagboard template. (See figure 2.8.) Illustrate the book and write a story or dictate it to the teacher. Use the key words for an independent writing experience.

Log Book

Columbus kept a log book detailing his voyages and experiences in the New World. Several books are available in which Columbus's story is told in his own words. *The Log of Christopher Columbus*, edited by Steve Lowe, is an excellent version for younger children. *I, Columbus*, edited by Peter Roop and Connie Roop, is ideal for older children. (See bibliography on page 34.) Keep a log book about daily experiences. Fold a 9-by-12-inch piece of construction paper in half for the cover and include five pages, one for each day of the week. Record the date and draw a picture to illustrate an experience from each day. Older children can write about their experiences.

Fig. 2.8. Ship shape book directions and pattern.

Materials:

Blue construction paper
Tagboard
White paper
Markers or pencils
Stapler
Key words

What to Do:

Trace two boat shapes from a tagboard template.

Cut out the ship shapes for the cover.

Teacher may precut the white pages.

Staple together the cover and white pages.

Illustrate and write a story about Columbus.

Use the key words for an independent writing experience.

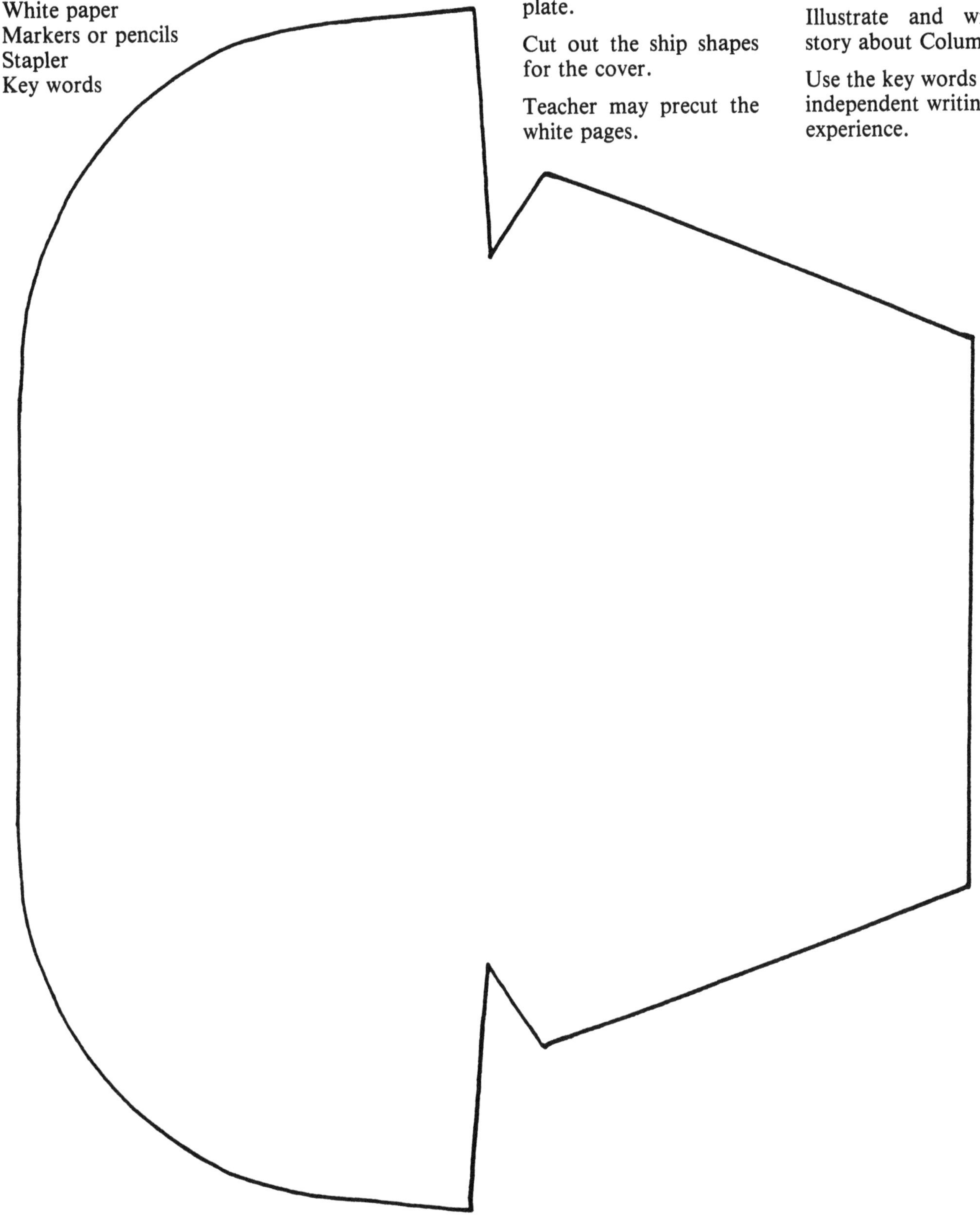

COOPERATIVE/GROUP EXPERIENCE

Outfit a Ship

Read "Ships and Sailing" in Ken Hills's *The Voyages of Columbus*. (See bibliography on page 34.) Discuss the kinds of food that were appropriate for the long voyages. Examples include beef jerky, cheese, honey, rice, nuts, or any type of dried foods. Have each child bring one such food item from home. Taste the different foods at snack time or as a group experience.

Mapmakers

Christopher Columbus learned to make maps from his brother Bartholomew. Both *Columbus: The Triumphant Failure* by Oliver Postgate and Naomi Linnell and Barry Smith's *The First Voyage of Christopher Columbus 1492* contain beautifully illustrated maps of Columbus's routes to the New World. Read about the history of mapmaking in *Maps and Globes* by Jack Knowlton. (See bibliography on page 34.)

To experience mapmaking, first brew 4 teabags in 1 cup of boiling water. Let tea bags steep for 10 minutes. Use cotton balls and rub the tea over a sheet of heavy white drawing paper. The tea will stain the paper, giving it an aged look. Allow the paper to dry. Use black, blue, brown, and green markers to make a map of the New World.

ART/CRAFT EXPERIENCE

Weavers

Columbus was determined to travel to faraway places instead of becoming a weaver like his father. Read *Christopher Columbus and His Voyage to the New World* by Robert Young. (See bibliography on page 35.) Become a weaver like Columbus's father. Use plastic yarn needles, yarn, and rug backing purchased from craft stores. Rug backing has a large open weave and plastic needles threaded with yarn can easily go through it. Weave the yarn through the rug backing to create your own weaving.

Tempera Painting

In Columbus's time, people believed that the ocean was filled with sea monsters and other terrible creatures. Peter Sis's *Follow the Dream* contains numerous illustrations of imaginary sea monsters. (See bibliography on page 35.) Create your own sea monsters using green, purple, blue, and yellow tempera paint. Write a caption for the sea monster painting. Display the paintings on the walls or the bulletin board. Bind the paintings together to make a class book.

Ocean Sea Mural

Examine and discuss the ocean paintings in Peter Sis's *Follow the Dream*. (See bibliography on page 35.) Use blue tempera cakes and water to paint an ocean sea mural. Use brown and green tempera cakes and water to paint islands in the ocean sea. While painting the ocean sea mural, listen to the music "Follow a Dream" by Pamela Copus and Joyce Harlow, from *Holiday Story Play Music*, or other suitable music. (See bibliography on page 35.)

Float Your Boat

Read *Boats* by Anne Rockwell for an informative account on boats. (See bibliography on page 35.) Make boats from small milk cartons cut in half lengthwise. Add a craft stick with a sail. (See figure 2.9.) Float the boats in a small dishpan of water.

Fig. 2.9. Float your boat directions.

Materials:	**What to Do:**
Milk carton	Cut milk carton in half lengthwise.
Scissors	
White paper	Cut a paper sail and glue on a craft stick.
Craft stick	
Pan with water	Glue the craft stick to the inside of the milk carton.
	Float your boat.

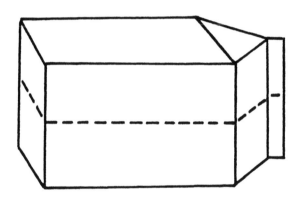

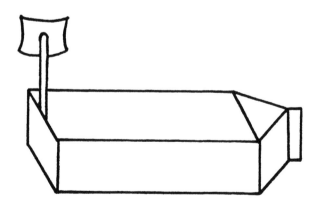

Treasure Chest

Make a treasure chest and fill it with the things you would take on an ocean voyage. (See figure 2.10.) Use markers to draw the artifacts or cut objects from magazines or catalogs and paste them inside the treasure chest.

Fig. 2.10. Treasure chest pattern and directions.

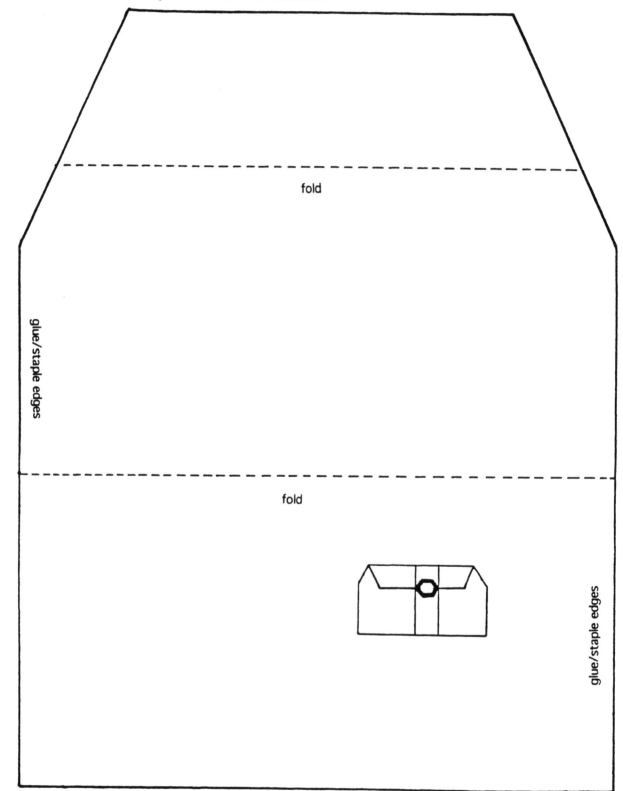

COOKING/MATH EXPERIENCE

Sea Biscuits

One of the food items taken on Columbus's voyages was sea biscuits. Make your own sea biscuits by following the recipe. (See figure 2.11.) Make, bake, and eat sea biscuits.

Fig. 2.11. Sea biscuits recipe.

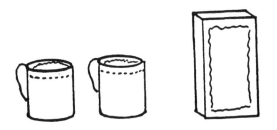 2 cups
biscuit mix

 ½ cup
water (stir)

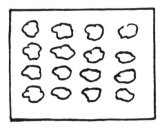 drop by
teaspoonful
on cookie sheet

bake at 450⁰ for 8-10 minutes

Banana Boats

Make banana boats of the Niña, the Pinta, or the Santa Maria. Cut a banana in half. Use a toothpick and a large marshmallow for the sail. Pretend to be sea monsters while eating the boats.

Dried Apples on a String

Because of the length of the voyages, only dried foods could be taken on the sea trips. Remove the core from six to eight apples. Run a string through the holes and tie to an oven rack. Cook on the lowest setting until the apples are dried. Remove the string, slice, and eat.

New World Food Tasting

Experience the foods Columbus found in the New World. Include sweet potatoes, pineapple, coconut, corn, cassova, groundnuts (peanuts), and french beans in the tasting experience. Make a graph to determine favorite New World foods.

Knots on a Rope

In Columbus's time, sailors used knots on a rope to determine how fast their ships were traveling. Use a clothesline cut in 18-inch lengths. Tie slip knots the length of the rope. Experience tying other kinds of knots. (See figure 2.12.) Count the number of knots on each rope.

Fig. 2.12. Knots on a rope illustrations and directions.

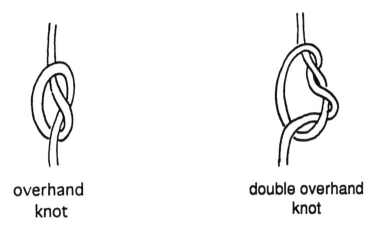

overhand
knot

double overhand
knot

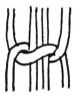

half knot

square knot

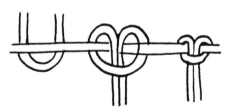

lark's head knot

SCIENCE/DISCOVERY EXPERIENCE

Discovery Museum

Create a discovery museum to display items and books about Christopher Columbus. Have the children contribute a variety of items, such as foods from the Old and New Worlds, model ships, flags, knots, compasses, and other collections. Display the items on a table or counter top in the classroom. Use sentence strips to label the items. Explore the museum with a group or individually and look at these everyday items in a new way.

Compass

Make a compass by stroking a large metal yarn needle against a magnet until the needle becomes magnetized. Push the needle through a small cork. Place the cork in a shallow dish of water. The needle will point in a north-south direction.

Spice Sampler

Columbus had planned to travel to India for spices. Experience the smell of spices such as allspice, cinnamon, clove, ginger, marjoram, mustard, nutmeg, paprika, pepper, rosemary, sage, and thyme. On a piece of 9-by-12-inch art paper, make circles using a glue stick. Sprinkle different spices onto the glue circles. Label with the names of the spices.

Frigate Birds

After several false sightings, Columbus realized land was near after seeing frigate birds. Because their feathers are not waterproof, frigate birds stay close to land. Make an origami frigate bird. (See figure 2.13.)

The Ocean Sea

Early sailors believed that only one ocean, the Ocean Sea, existed, and they thought it was inhabited by sea monsters. *Sea Monsters of Long Ago* by Millicent E. Selsam describes the ancient sea creatures that existed in prehistoric times. *The Sailor's Book* by Charlotte Agell explores the idea that the sea is a dragon. (See bibliography on page 34.) Create an ocean sea by using a small plastic swimming pool. Place rocks, plastic monsters, and three plastic sailboats in the swimming pool. Fill with enough water so that the sailboats will float. Experience sailing around the rocks and monsters.

Fig. 2.13. Frigate bird illustrations and directions.

Cut paper 8½" X 8½";
fold in half and crease;
unfold

fold edges in to
center crease

fold over

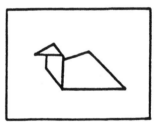

fold up

fold down

glue on blue paper

MUSIC/GAME EXPERIENCE

Native American Ball Game

According to Ken Hills's *The Voyages of Columbus*, the Arawaks, a Native American people, played a ball game in which two teams tried to knock a ball over their opponent's goal line.

Mark a playing field with a goal line at each end. Divide into two teams. While one team stands behind and guards its line, the other team must try to kick a ball over its opponent's goal line. Take turns trying to kick the ball over the goal lines.

Columbus, Columbus

Place a small treasure chest under an empty chair. The child selected to be Columbus sits in the chair with his or her back to the rest of the group and with eyes closed tight. Select a pirate to quietly sneak up on Columbus and steal a trinket from the treasure chest. The pirate returns to the group and hides the trinket. Chant in unison:

> Columbus, Columbus,
> sitting there,
> Who stole the treasure
> from under your chair?

Columbus turns around and tries to guess who the pirate is. After three guesses, the pirate gets to be Columbus and sits in the chair. The game continues until all the children have participated.

Capture the Flag

Divide the class into two opposing teams. One team can be Spain and the other team can be the Native Americans. Use two handkerchiefs or scarves for the flags. Divide the field of battle in the middle. Each team tries to steal the other side's flag and take it back to their side. If a team member is tagged in the process, then he or she must go to an area designated as the jail. Captives may be freed from jail if their teammates can tag them without being caught. The game continues until a flag is captured.

BIBLIOGRAPHY

Agell, Charlotte. *The Sailor's Book*. Willowdale, Ontario, Canada: Firefly Books, 1991.

Columbus, Christopher. *I, Columbus*. Edited by Peter Roop and Connie Roop. New York: Walker, 1990.

Fritz, Jean. *The Great Adventure of Christopher Columbus*. New York: Putnam & Grosset, 1992.

Greene, Carol. *Christopher Columbus: A Great Explorer*. Chicago: Childrens Press, 1989.

Hills, Ken. *The Voyages of Columbus*. New York: Random House, 1991.

Knowlton, Jack. *Maps and Globes*. New York: Harper Trophy, 1985.

Lowe, Steve. *The Log of Christopher Columbus.* New York: Philomel Books, 1992.

Marzollo, Jean. *In 1492.* New York: Scholastic, 1991.

Postgate, Oliver, and Naomi Linnell. *Columbus: The Triumphant Failure.* New York: Watts, 1991.

Rockwell, Anne. *Boats.* New York: E. P. Dutton, 1982.

Selsam, Millicent E. *Sea Monsters of Long Ago.* New York: Four Winds Press, 1977.

Sis, Peter. *Follow the Dream.* New York: Alfred A. Knopf, 1991.

Smith, Barry. *The First Voyage of Christopher Columbus 1492.* New York: Viking, 1992.

Yolen, Jane. *Encounter.* San Diego, CA: Harcourt Brace Jovanovich, 1992.

Young, Robert. *Christopher Columbus and His Voyage to the New World.* Englewood Cliffs, NJ: Silver Press, 1990.

Music

Copus, Pamela, and Joyce Harlow. "Follow a Dream." *Holiday Story Play Music.* Plano, TX: Dreamtime Productions, P.O. Box 940061, Plano, TX 75094-0061.

CHAPTER

3

THANKSGIVING

DRAMA/PLAY EXPERIENCE

Read *Three Young Pilgrims* by Cheryl Harness to introduce the theme of Thanksgiving Day. (See bibliography on page 52.) *Three Young Pilgrims* is a true account of Bartholomew, Remember, and Mary Allerton, young Pilgrim children who sailed on the *Mayflower*. The illustrations and text detail their story from the landing at Plymouth through the first Thanksgiving feast. Demonstrate the simpletees costumes and play props.

Simpletees Costumes

Use simpletees costumes of Bartholomew, Remember, and Mary for a dramatic play experience. (See figures 3.1 and 3.2.)

Play Props

Play props can include plastic ears of corn, pumpkins, gourds, nuts, a white apron, dishes, and a tablecloth to use for dramatizing a Thanksgiving feast.

Face Masks

Create face masks of Bartholomew, Remember, and Mary. Illustrate the masks with facial features for the various characters. (See figures 3.3, 3.4, and 3.5.)

Stick Puppets/Paper Bag Theater

Make stick puppets of Bartholomew, Remember, and Mary. (See figure 3.6.) Create a paper bag theater for the stick puppets and present a story about Thanksgiving to a friend or families. (See figure 1.5 on page 6.)

(Text continues on page 43.)

Fig. 3.1. Simpletees costumes: Thanksgiving.

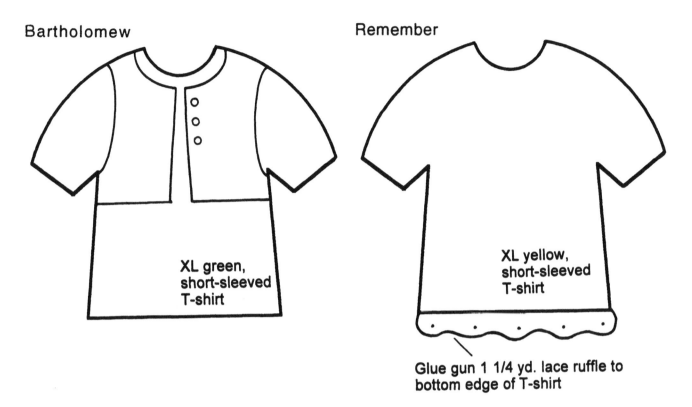

Bartholomew

XL green,
short-sleeved
T-shirt

Remember

XL yellow,
short-sleeved
T-shirt

Glue gun 1 1/4 yd. lace ruffle to
bottom edge of T-shirt

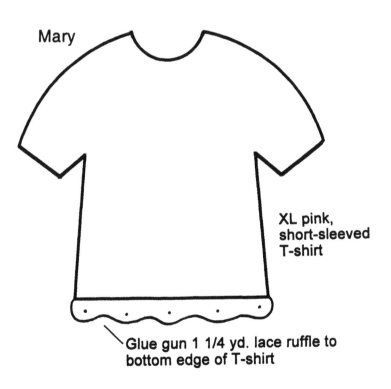

Mary

XL pink,
short-sleeved
T-shirt

Glue gun 1 1/4 yd. lace ruffle to
bottom edge of T-shirt

Fig. 3.2. Vest directions and illustrations.

Materials:

½ yard grey craft felt
Scissors
3 buttons
Glue gun

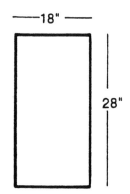

What to Do:

Cut grey felt 18" X 28".

Fold in half and cut out neck opening.

Cut front opening.

Glue gun sides 4" up from the bottom.

Glue gun 3 buttons.

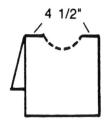

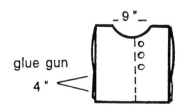

Fig. 3.3. Bartholomew face mask pattern.

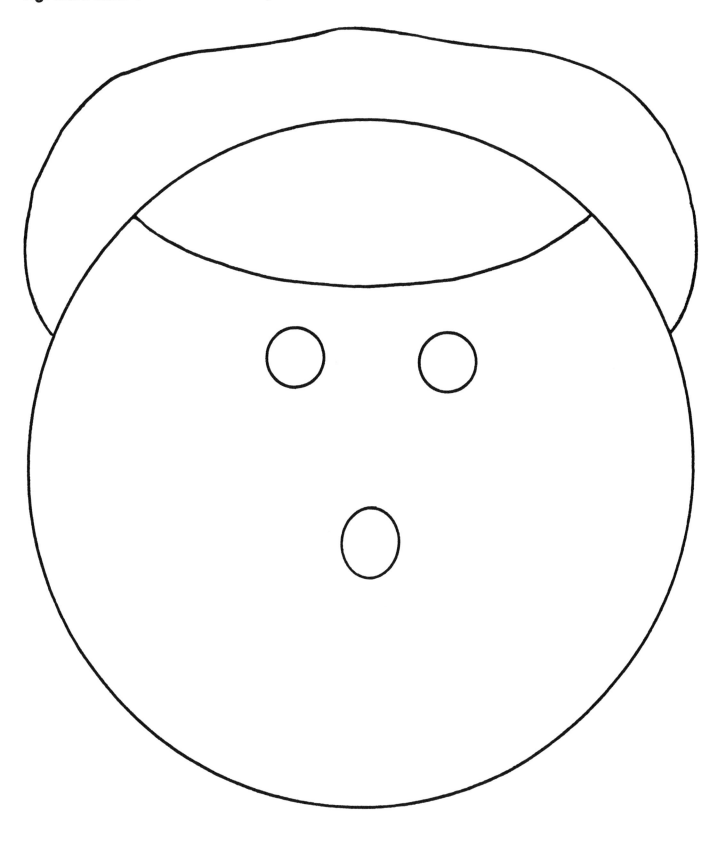

Fig. 3.4. Remember face mask pattern.

Fig. 3.5. Mary face mask pattern.

Fig. 3.6. Stick puppet patterns: Thanksgiving.

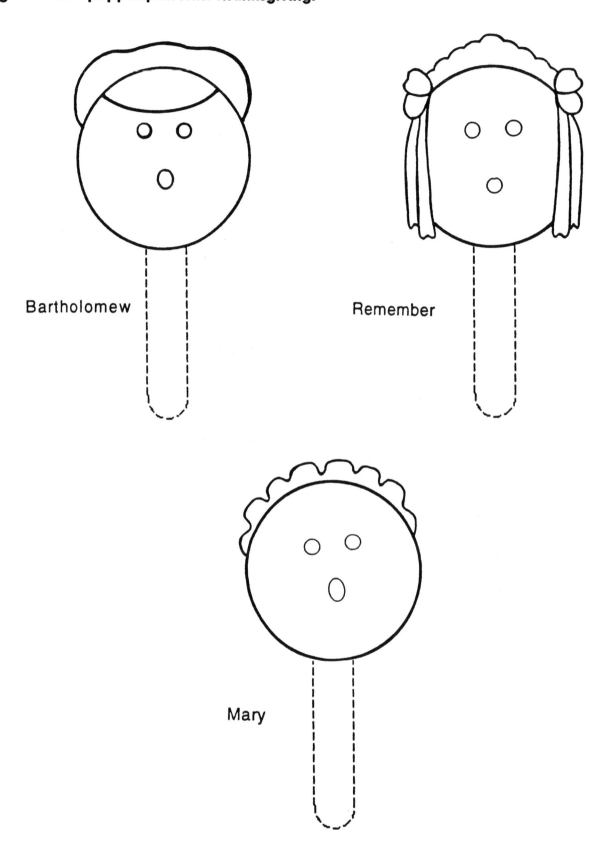

Bartholomew

Remember

Mary

LITERATURE/WRITING EXPERIENCE

Thanksgiving *Versions*

Read a variety of stories about Thanksgiving. Gail Gibbons's *Thanksgiving Day* offers an easily understood description of how we came to celebrate the Thanksgiving holiday. *Thanksgiving* by Miriam Nerlove and Steven Kroll's *Oh, What a Thanksgiving!* compare the first Thanksgiving with our present-day celebrations. (See bibliography on page 52.)

Thanksgiving *Children's Version*

After experiencing the different stories about Thanksgiving, write a children's version about their Thanksgiving celebrations on a large sheet of chart paper.

Key-Word Books and Key Words

Make a key-word book with the unique or important words from *Three Young Pilgrims* by Cheryl Harness. (See bibliography on page 52.) The key words for *Three Young Pilgrims* are as follows:

Bartholomew	Remember	Mary
Thanksgiving	*Mayflower*	Plymouth
Pilgrim	November	pumpkin
corn		

Pilgrim Hat Shape Book

A variety of books give detailed accounts of the Pilgrim's saga. *The Pilgrims of Plimoth* by Marcia Sewall vividly describes the Pilgrims' journey and first year in Plymouth. Kate Waters's *Sarah Morton's Day* gives a photographic portrayal of a young Pilgrim girl's life at Plymouth Colony. ... *If You Sailed on the Mayflower in 1620* by Ann McGovern describes life aboard ship and on shore. (See bibliography on page 52.) Make a pilgrim hat shape book by tracing the pilgrim hat shape from a tagboard template. (See figure 3.7.) Illustrate and write a story about the Pilgrims or dictate it to the teacher. Use the key words for an independent writing experience.

Thanksgiving Invitation

In *Chester Chipmunk's Thanksgiving* by Barbara Williams, Chester thoughtfully invites Cousin Archie to Thanksgiving dinner, with humorous consequences. (See bibliography on page 52.) Write an invitation to a friend or family member to have a Thanksgiving snack with you.

Fig. 3.7. Pilgrim hat shape book directions and pattern.

Materials:

Black construction paper   Scissors
Tagboard   Stapler
White paper   Markers or pencils
                                  Key words

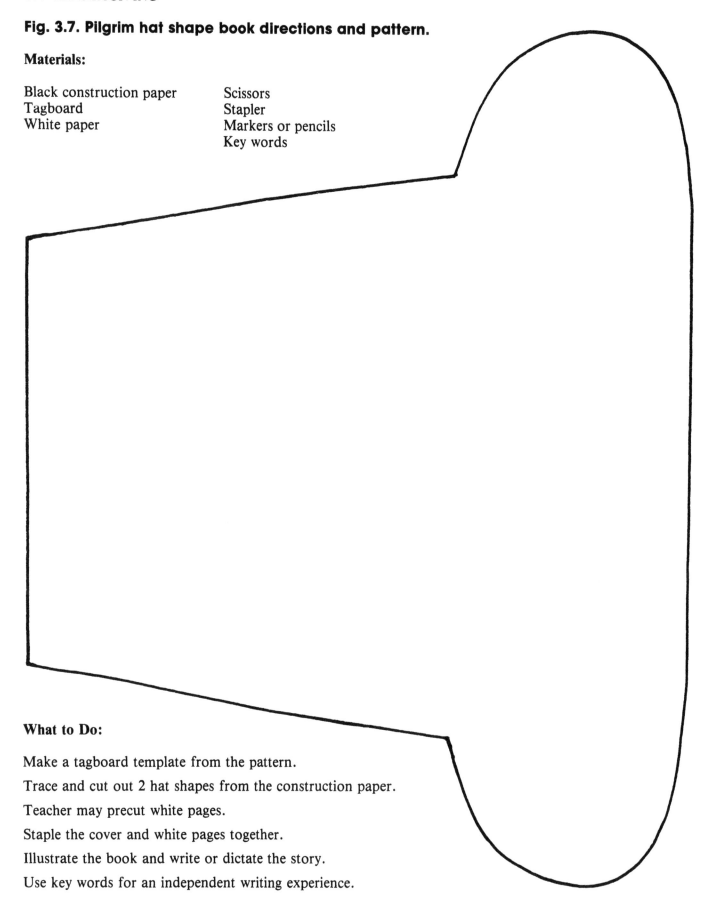

What to Do:

Make a tagboard template from the pattern.

Trace and cut out 2 hat shapes from the construction paper.

Teacher may precut white pages.

Staple the cover and white pages together.

Illustrate the book and write or dictate the story.

Use key words for an independent writing experience.

COOPERATIVE/GROUP EXPERIENCE

Turkey Parade

In *'Twas the Night Before Thanksgiving* by Dav Pilkey, a group of school children takes a field trip to a turkey farm and ends up saving the turkeys from becoming Thanksgiving dinner. (See bibliography on page 52.) Make turkey feet and a turkey vest by tracing the turkey feet shape and the feather pattern from tagboard templates. (See figures 3.8, 3.9, and 3.10.) Wear the turkey feet and vest while having a turkey parade.

Pumpkin Patch

Pumpkins by Mary Lyn Ray is about a field, a man who lives by the field, and what he does to save the field from building development. (See bibliography on page 52.) Create a pumpkin patch for the classroom by stuffing brown lunch bags with newspaper. Twist the top of each bag and secure with masking tape. Paint the pumpkin portion of the bag with orange tempera paint and the stem with green tempera paint. Use green crepe paper to make tendrils. Display the pumpkins in a patch or attach to a bulletin board.

(Text continues on page 48.)

Fig. 3.8. Turkey vest directions and pattern.

Materials:

Large grocery bag
Scissors
Stapler
Glue
Paper feathers (see figure 3.9)

What to Do:

Push out sides of bag to flatten.

Staple bottom of bag to make vest flat instead of boxy.

Cut out armholes. (See illustration.)

Cut V-neck opening.

Cut center front open.

Glue feathers to the vest.

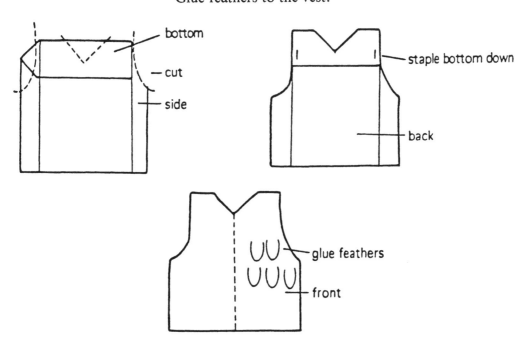

Fig. 3.9. Turkey feather pattern.

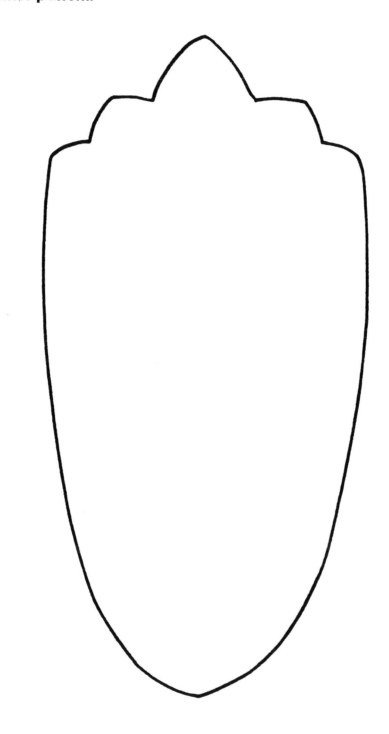

Fig. 3.10. Turkey feet directions and pattern.

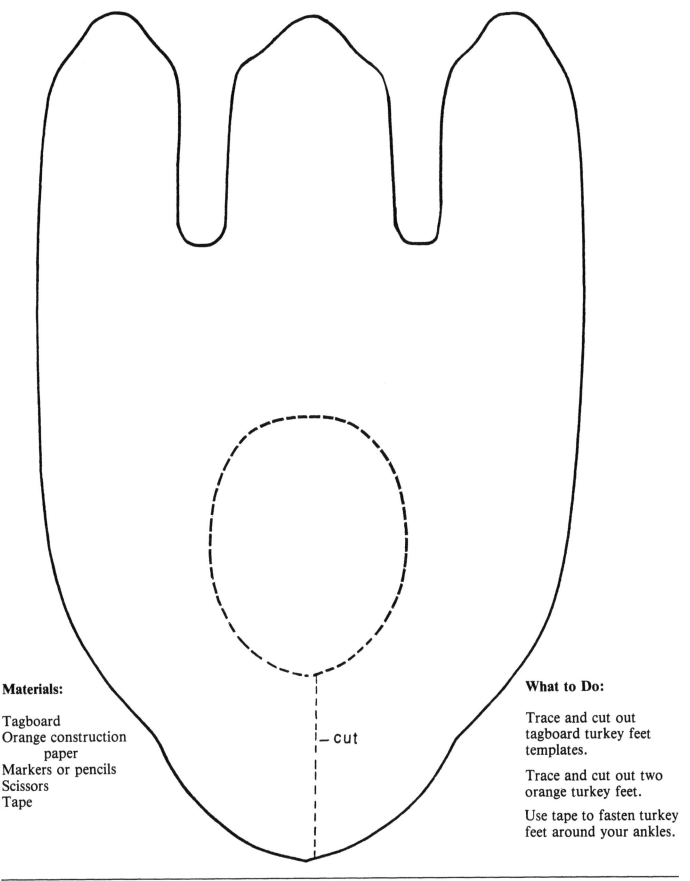

— cut

Materials:

Tagboard
Orange construction
    paper
Markers or pencils
Scissors
Tape

What to Do:

Trace and cut out
tagboard turkey feet
templates.

Trace and cut out two
orange turkey feet.

Use tape to fasten turkey
feet around your ankles.

ART/CRAFT EXPERIENCE

Tempera Painting

In *Turkey's Gift to the People* by Ani Rucki, Mr. and Mrs. Turkey remember to bring along the seeds all the animals will need to start over after a great flood. (See bibliography on page 52.) Paint a picture of a turkey using brown, orange, and red tempera. Display the paintings on the wall or the bulletin board. Bind the paintings together to make a class book.

Native American Makeup

Berries, tree bark, and fruit were used by the Native Americans for making paint. The decorations and colors they used on their bodies and faces had various meanings. Decorate faces with Native American makeup. Combine 4 teaspoons of white shortening, 10 teaspoons of corn starch, and 2 teaspoons of white flour. Add 8 drops of glycerin. Separate the mixture in half and add a few drops of red and yellow food coloring to each portion. Paint faces with the red and yellow makeup.

Corncob Printing

In *Corn Is Maize* by Aliki, facts ranging from the discovery of corn by the Native Americans to its present-day uses are delightfully presented. (See bibliography on page 52.) Make corncob prints by letting corncobs dry out for several days. Pour a thin layer of tempera paint into a shallow tray and roll the cobs in the paint. Roll the corncobs across a piece of paper to make a corncob print.

COOKING/MATH EXPERIENCE

Thanksgiving Feast

The first Thanksgiving feast is wonderfully illustrated in *N. C. Wyeth's Pilgrims* by Robert San Souci. (See bibliography on page 52.) Celebrate Thanksgiving with a feast of apple cider, beef jerky, popcorn, cranberries, and pumpkin pie. Make a graph to determine favorite Thanksgiving foods.

Ten Little Rabbits

Read *Ten Little Rabbits* by Virginia Grossman and Sylvia Long, a counting book that is illustrated with rabbits as members of many of the Native American cultures found in America. (See bibliography on page 52.) Make a blanket repeat design or pattern similar to the illustrations in the back of the book. Use bingo markers to create the designs and patterns on 12-by-18-inch sheets of art paper.

Cranberry Sauce

The making of a very fat Thanksgiving turkey is detailed in *Sometimes It's Turkey—Sometimes It's Feathers* by Lorna Balian. (See bibliography on page 52.) Make cranberry sauce for a Thanksgiving snack by following the recipe. (See figure 3.11.)

Fig. 3.11. Cranberry sauce recipe.

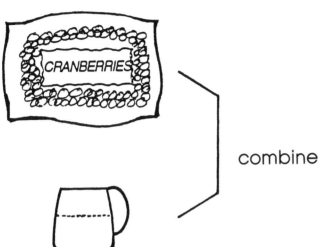

1 package fresh cranberries

combine

½ cup water

bring to a boil

add 2 cups sugar simmer 10-15 minutes until thick

Pilgrim Bread Pudding

Make Pilgrim bread pudding by soaking 5 cups of diced bread, with the crust removed, in 3 cups milk. Combine 3 eggs with ½ cup sugar. Add ½ cup raisins and ½ teaspoon nutmeg. Stir all the ingredients together and pour into a baking dish. Place the dish in a pan of hot water and bake for 45 minutes at 300°.

Cornmeal Measuring

Corn is Maize by Aliki tells about cornmeal, one of the many products made from corn. (See bibliography on page 52.) Place cornmeal in a dishpan. Use measuring cups, scoops, and funnels to measure and pour the cornmeal.

SCIENCE/DISCOVERY EXPERIENCE

Discovery Museum

Create a discovery museum to display items and books about corn. Have the children contribute a variety of corn and corn products, such as ears of fresh corn, dried Indian corn, popcorn kernels, popped corn, canned corn, cornmeal, corn oil, corn flakes, and corn chips. Plant kernels of corn in a sealed plastic bag with a small layer of dirt. Experience grinding corn as the Native Americans did by using a metate (slightly hollowed grinding base) and grinding stone. Display the items on a table, shelf, or counter top in the classroom. Use sentence strips to label the items. Explore the museum as a group or individually and look at corn in a new way.

Pumpkin Pumpkin

Read *The Pumpkin Patch* by Elizabeth King, a book of photographs documenting the life cycle of the pumpkin. (See bibliography on page 52.) Experience the delight of cutting open a pumpkin and scooping out the seeds. Plant some of the pumpkin seeds in a plastic bag with a small layer of dirt. Close the bag and hang it in a window so that the seeds will sprout. Clean the remaining pumpkins seeds and toast them for a Thanksgiving treat.

Seed Cataloging

Seeds are significant in *Turkey's Gift to the People* by Ani Rucki and *Mousekin's Thanksgiving* by Edna Miller. (See bibliography on page 52.) Create a seed catalog by purchasing seeds at a nursery or through a seed mail-order company. Remove the seeds from the packages and place both the package and the seeds in a sealed plastic bag. Display the bags on a bulletin board so that they can be easily examined.

MUSIC/GAME EXPERIENCE

Hide the Thimble

"Hide the Thimble" was a game that Pilgrim children played. One child is selected to hide a thimble while the remaining children hide their eyes. The children then look for the thimble until it is found. Whovever finds the thimble hides it again so that the game can continue. As a variation, an ear of corn can be substituted for the thimble.

Pumpkin Race

In *Pumpkin Pumpkin* by Jeanne Titherington, a little boy discovers the life cycle of the pumpkin. (See bibliography on page 52.) Have a pumpkin race to celebrate the Thanksgiving holiday. Each child who is racing will need a miniature pumpkin and a wooden spoon. Children push the pumpkins over a course with the spoons.

Turkey in the Straw

Pretend to be a turkey in hiding on Thanksgiving Day by singing "Turkey in the Straw" from *Holiday Story Play Music* by Pamela Copus and Joyce Harlow. (See bibliography on page 52.)

Turkey in the Straw

Turkey in the straw,
Turkey in the hay,
Come out, little turkey,
It's Thanksgiving Day.

Turkey in the straw,
Turkey in the hay,
Come out, little turkey,
I must eat you today!

No turkey in the straw
No turkey in the hay,
My fat little turkey
Has run, run away.

Come back little turkey,
Come back right away,
Tomorrow's too late,
I must eat you today!

Turkey in the straw,
Turkey in the hay,
Come out, little turkey,
It's Thanksgiving Day!

Joyce Harlow

BIBLIOGRAPHY

Aliki. *Corn Is Maize*. New York: Harper Trophy, 1976.

Balian, Lorna. *Sometimes It's Turkey—Sometimes It's Feathers*. Nashville, TN: Abingdon Press, 1973.

Gibbons, Gail. *Thanksgiving Day*. New York: Holiday House, 1983.

Grossman, Virginia, and Sylvia Long. *Ten Little Rabbits*. San Francisco: Chronicle Books, 1991.

Harness, Cheryl. *Three Young Pilgrims*. New York: Bradbury Press, 1992.

King, Elizabeth. *The Pumpkin Patch*. New York: Dutton Children's Books, 1990.

Kroll, Steven. *Oh, What a Thanksgiving!* New York: Scholastic, 1988.

McGovern, Ann. *...If You Sailed on the Mayflower in 1620*. New York: Scholastic, 1969.

Miller, Edna. *Mousekin's Thanksgiving*. New York: Simon & Schuster, 1985.

Nerlove, Miriam. *Thanksgiving*. Niles, Il: Albert Whitman, 1990.

Pilkey, Dav. *'Twas the Night Before Thanksgiving*. New York: Orchard Books, 1990.

Ray, Mary Lyn. *Pumpkins*. San Diego, CA: Harcourt Brace Jovanovich, 1992.

Rucki, Ani. *Turkey's Gift to the People*. Flagstaff, AZ: Northland, 1992.

San Souci, Robert. *N. C. Wyeth's Pilgrims*. San Francisco: Chronicle Books, 1991.

Sewall, Marcia. *The Pilgrims of Plimoth*. New York: Atheneum, 1986.

Titherington, Jeanne. *Pumpkin Pumpkin*. New York: Scholastic, 1986.

Waters, Kate. *Sarah Morton's Day*. New York: Scholastic, 1989.

Williams, Barbara. *Chester Chipmunk's Thanksgiving*. New York: E. P. Dutton, 1978.

Music

Copus, Pamela, and Joyce Harlow. "Turkey in the Straw." *Holiday Story Play Music*. Plano, TX: Dreamtime Productions, P.O. Box 940061, Plano, TX 75094-0061.

CHAPTER 4

CHRISTMAS

DRAMA/PLAY EXPERIENCE

Read Bernadette Watts's version of *The Elves and the Shoemaker* to introduce the theme of Christmas. (See bibliography on page 70.) In this retelling of the story by the Brothers Grimm, two little elves surprise a poor but honest shoemaker by making two pairs of shoes out of leather that was enough for only one pair. Demonstrate the simpletees costumes and play props.

Simpletees Costumes

Use the simpletees costumes of the shoemaker, his wife, and the two elves for a dramatic play experience. (See figures 4.1 and 4.2 in addition to figure 3.2, page 38, for the vest pattern.)

Play Props

Play props can include a shoeshine kit, small aprons, pairs of small shoes, clear shoe wax, a toothbrush to apply shoe wax, and flannel squares to shine the shoes.

Face Masks

Create face masks of the shoemaker, his wife, and the two elves. Use tagboard templates and trace the different characters. (See figures 4.3, 4.4, and 4.5.)

Stick Puppets/Paper Bag Theater

Make stick puppets of the shoemaker, his wife, and the two elves. (See figure 4.6.) Create a paper bag theater for the stick puppets. (See figure 1.5 on page 6.) Present the story of the shoemaker and the elves to a friend, or take home and present to parents.

(Text continues on page 60.)

Fig. 4.1. Simpletees costumes: Christmas.

Shoemaker

Wife

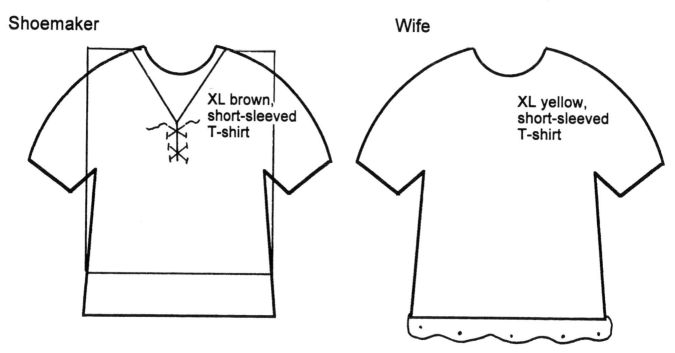

XL brown, short-sleeved T-shirt

XL yellow, short-sleeved T-shirt

Glue gun 1 1/4 yd. lace ruffle to bottom of T-shirt

Elf

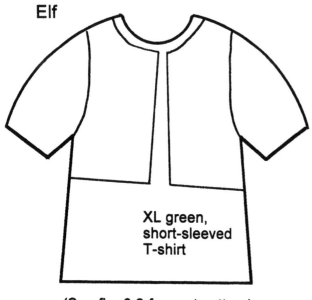

XL green, short-sleeved T-shirt

(See fig. 3.2 for vest pattern)

Fig. 4.2. Shoemaker tunic directions and illustrations.

Materials:

½ yard brown craft felt
1 42" yellow shoelace
Scissors
Glue gun

What to Do:

Cut 20" X 48" brown felt.

Fold felt in half and cut a V-neck opening.

Cut a 3" slit on the front of the V-neck opening.

Cut 4 slits on each side of the front neck opening.

Thread a shoelace through the slits and tie.

Glue gun sides of tunic together 10" down from shoulder to form armholes.

Wear tunic over an XL T-shirt.

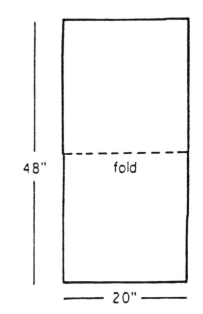

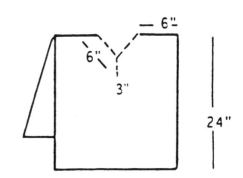

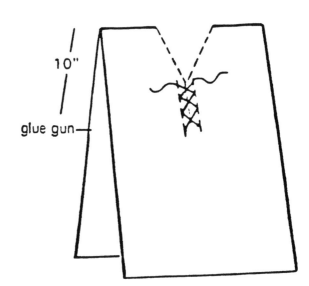

Fig. 4.3. Shoemaker face mask pattern.

Fig. 4.4. Wife face mask pattern.

Fig. 4.5. Elf face mask pattern.

Fig. 4.6. Elves and shoemaker stick puppets.

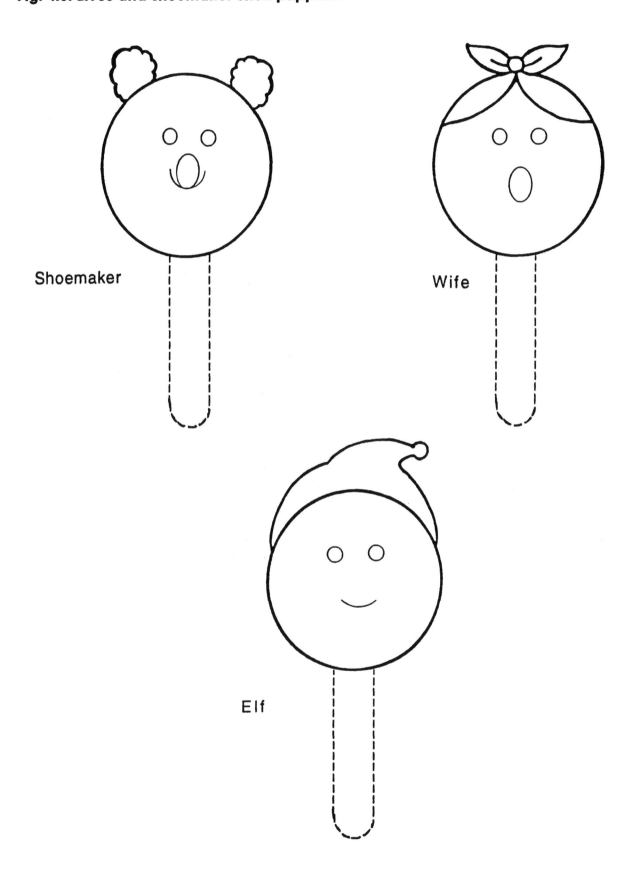

Shoemaker

Wife

Elf

LITERATURE/WRITING EXPERIENCE

The Elves and the Shoemaker *Versions*

Experience the various versions of the Brothers Grimm's "The Elves and the Shoemaker." *The Elves and the Shoemaker* by Paul Galdone, Freya Littledale's *The Elves and the Shoemaker* and *The Shoemaker and the Elves* by Ilse Plume uniquely illustrate this familiar tale. (See bibliography on page 69.)

The Elves and the Shoemaker *Children's Version*

Write a children's version about "The Shoemaker and the Elves" on a large sheet of chart paper.

Key-Word Books and Key Words

Make a key-word book with the unique or important words from "The Shoemaker and the Elves." The key words for "The Shoemaker and the Elves" are as follows:

elves	Christmas	money
shoemaker	wife	cobbler
shoes	leather	customer

Tree Shape Book

Make an tree shape book by tracing the tree shape from a tagboard template. (See figure 4.7.) Illustrate the book and write a story or dictate it to the teacher. Use the key words for an independent writing experience.

Christmas Mailboxes

Read *The Jolly Christmas Postman* by Janet Ahlberg and Allan Ahlberg. (See bibliography on page 69.) In this book, the jolly postman delivers special Christmas greetings to numerous fairy-tale characters. Create Christmas mailboxes by using empty boxes with compartments. Empty liquor boxes are ideal, but be sure to cover them with decorative wrap or contact paper. Label each compartment with a child's name. Write letters to each other and put in the correct mail slots.

Christmas Wishes

In Margaret Wise Brown's *On Christmas Eve*, the children sneak out of bed on Christmas Eve to touch the Christmas tree and make a wish. (See bibliography on page 69.) Write a wish for Christmas on a small strip of paper. Tie your wish to a tree either inside or outside.

Fig. 4.7. Tree shape book directions and pattern.

Materials:

Green construction paper
Tagboard
White paper
Scissors
Stapler
Markers or pencils
Key words

What to Do:

Make a tagboard template from the pattern.

Trace and cut out 2 tree shapes from the construction paper.

Teacher may precut white pages.

Staple the cover and white pages together.

Illustrate the book and write or dictate the story.

Use key words for an independent writing experience.

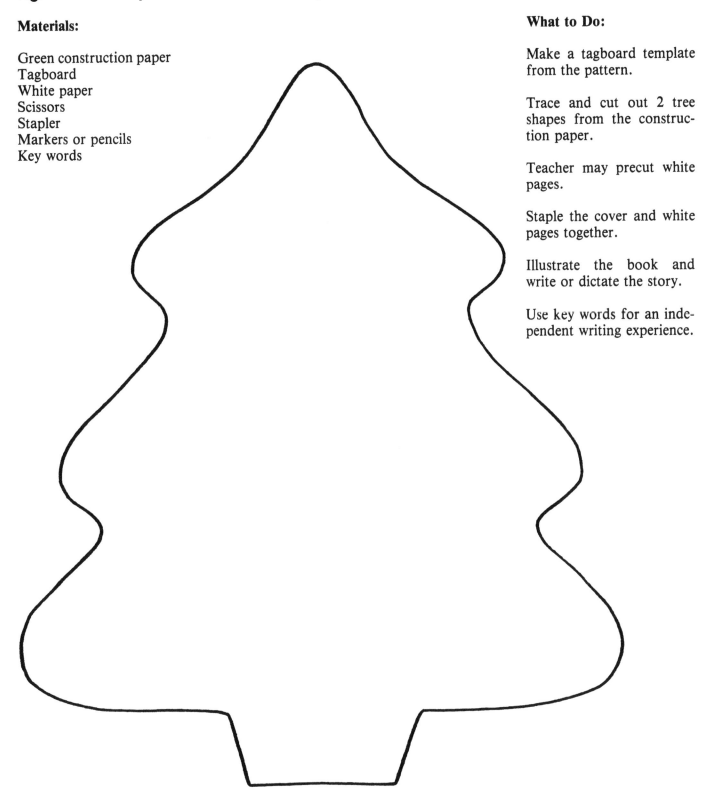

Envelope Wish Book

Make an envelope wish book. (See figure 4.8.) Draw a picture of what you want for Christmas and place the drawing inside an envelope. Combine the pages and bind them together for a class wish book.

Fig. 4.8. Wish book directions and illustration.

Materials:

8½" X 11" white paper
Letter-size envelopes
Glue stick
Scissors
Note-size paper
Markers or pencils
Stapler

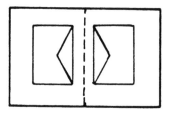 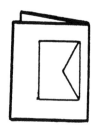

What to Do:

Fold the white paper in half.

Glue an envelope on each side of the folded paper.

Cut off the glue strip from the envelope flap.

Draw or write your Christmas wish and insert it in an envelope page.

Staple the pages together to make a Christmas wish book.

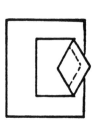

COOPERATIVE/GROUP EXPERIENCE

Gift Shop

Read Jan Brett's *The Wild Christmas Reindeer*. (See bibliography on page 69.) Brett's illustrations not only show the story of Teeka and the reindeer but also detail the elves' preparations for Christmas. Set up a Christmas gift shop with small Christmas ornaments, toys, note pads, a telephone, a cash register, and shopping bags.

Gift-Wrapping Factory

Wrapping and unwrapping presents is a favorite Christmas activity at any age. *On Christmas Eve* by Margaret Wise Brown describes the excitement presents around the Christmas tree bring to the young children. (See bibliography on page 69.) Provide small squares of gift wrap, tape, bows, and boxes to use in a classroom gift-wrapping factory.

Christmas Alphabet

Enjoy Christmas from the past by reading *A Christmas Alphabet* by Carolyn Wells. (See bibliography on page 70.) Create a class Christmas alphabet book. Work in small groups and illustrate the letters with various Christmas scenes. Combine the pages to make a Christmas alphabet book.

ART/CRAFT EXPERIENCE

Tempera Painting

In Hans Christian Andersen's *The Fir Tree*, a little fir tree wants to become a Christmas tree. (See bibliography on page 69.) Paint fir trees using green, white, and brown tempera paint. Display the paintings on the walls or the bulletin board. Bind the paintings together to make a classroom big book.

Christmas Cobwebs

Read Shirley Climo's *The Cobweb Christmas* to discover why tinsel is hung on Christmas trees. (See bibliography on page 69.) Make Christmas cobwebs by using white glue. Squeeze the bottle so that the glue makes a squiggle on a plastic lid. Sprinkle it with glitter and let the glue dry. Peel the glue off when it is dry and hang it in a window or on a small tree.

Christmas Stars

Patricia Polacco's *Uncle Vova's Tree* tells the story of the celebration of Christmas in the Russian tradition. (See bibliography on page 70.) Make Christmas stars similar to the children's in this story. (See figure 4.9.) Have a parade with your stars.

Fig. 4.9. Christmas star directions and pattern.

Materials:

Tagboard
Assorted colors of
     construction paper
Scissors
Glitter glue
Ribbon streamers
Tape or glue
Drinking straws

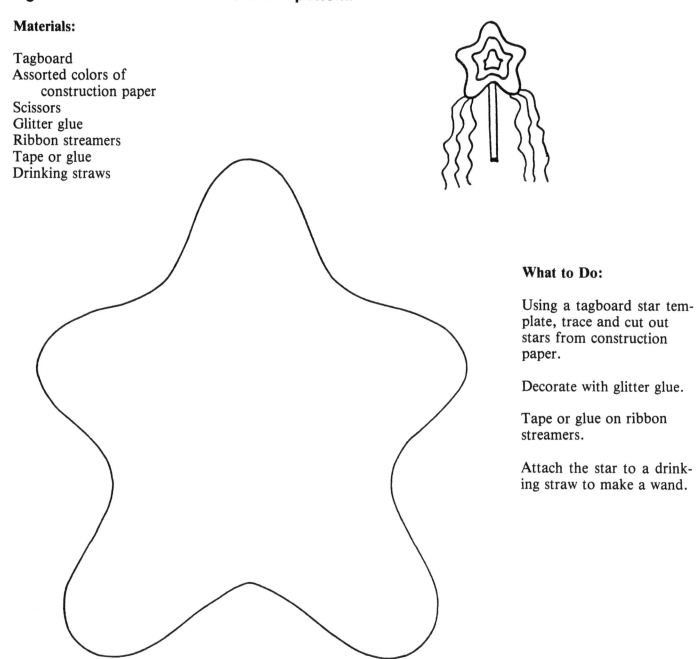

What to Do:

Using a tagboard star template, trace and cut out stars from construction paper.

Decorate with glitter glue.

Tape or glue on ribbon streamers.

Attach the star to a drinking straw to make a wand.

Snowflakes

Hear the sounds of Christmas while reading *The Snow Speaks* by Nancy White Carlstrom. (See bibliography on page 69.) Create a festive feeling by making snowflakes to display in windows or hang from the ceilings. Use 4-by-4-inch white paper. Fold the paper into fourths and cut out designs along the folds.

Nutcrackers

A favorite Christmas tradition is "The Nutcracker" by Tchaikovsky. *The Story of the Nutcracker Ballet* by Deborah Hautzig tells the story behind the ballet and the music. (See bibliography on page 69.) Make nutcrackers by using round cardboard tubes or containers. (See figure 4.10.) Use a nutcracker and crack assorted nuts for a nutritious snack.

Fig. 4.10. Nutcracker directions and illustration.

Materials:	**What to Do:**
Cylinder containers or toilet paper rolls	Paint cylinder with red and blue tempera.
Red, blue, and black tempera	Use black tempera for features.
White cotton balls	
Glue	Glue on cotton ball beard.

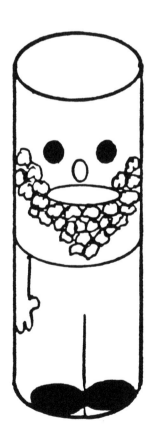

COOKING/MATH EXPERIENCE

Twelve Days of Snack

Read Claire Counihan's *The Twelve Days of Christmas*, a retelling of the traditional song. (See bibliography on page 69.) Beginning with the twelfth day before Christmas or winter break, use snack time as a countdown of the days. For example, on the first day before Christmas, count out one item for a snack. On the second day, count out two items. Continue until the twelfth day, when twelve items will be counted our for a snack.

Latkes

In Gloria Teles Pushker's *Toby Belfer Never Had a Christmas Tree*, a young girl tells the significance of Hanukkah and Jewish traditions to her Christian friends. (See bibliography on page 70.) Conclude the reading of this story by making and eating latkes. Use the recipe in figure 4.11.

Advent Chain

Twinkle, Twinkle, Little Star by Jane Taylor is the original version of the traditional English nursery rhyme. (See bibliography on page 70.) Make an Advent chain to count down the 25 days until Christmas. Begin with a yellow construction-paper star with the number 25 printed on it. Glue the ends of 1-by-6-inch strips of red and green construction paper and add a link to the chain to mark off each day.

Sugar Plums

Make sugar plums from dried apricots, dates, and pitted prunes. Cut the dried fruit in half lengthwise. Place a small cube of cream cheese on one of the halves. Press the fruit halves together to form a little sandwich, with the cream cheese in the middle. Roll the fruit in sugar and eat.

Fig. 4.11. Latkes recipe.

grate 6 medium potatoes

beat 6 eggs

chop 2 onions

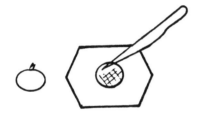

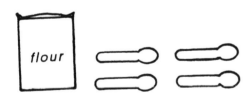

add 4 tablespoons flour

Combine ingredients and drop by tablespoonful into a frying pan of hot oil. Fry about 2 minutes on each side. Remove from hot oil and drain on paper towels. Serve with applesauce.

SCIENCE/DISCOVERY EXPERIENCE

Discovery Museum

Create a discovery museum to display items and books about Christmas and other winter holidays, such as Hanukkah. Have children contribute a variety of items, such as Christmas ornaments and decorations, holiday plants, and Advent calendars. A menorah, dreidels, nuts, and gold-covered chocolate candy can be displayed for Hanukkah. Display the contributions on a table, shelf, or counter top in the classroom. Use sentence strips to label the items. Explore the museum with the group or individually to discover both familiar and unique aspects of winter celebrations.

Christmas Rose

The Legend of the Christmas Rose by Ellin Greene is the retelling of a traditional Swedish folktale. (See bibliography on page 69.) In Goinge Forest, a beautiful garden blooms every Christmas Eve in remembrance of the birth of the Christ child. The Christmas rose is a member of the buttercup family and is not a true rose at all. The pale white flower grows from the cold winter earth. Plant amaryllis or paperwhite narcissus bulbs in clear plastic cups filled with potting soil. Follow the directions on the bulb package for proper planting procedures and care.

Rosemary

Read "The Rosemary Legend" from Tasha Tudor's *Take Joy! The Tasha Tudor Christmas Book*. (See bibliography on page 70.) Make rosemary sachets for a present for mothers or other special adults. (See page 150 for directions on making sachets.)

The Bird Tree

Read "The Bird Tree" from Tasha Tudor's *Take Joy! The Tasha Tudor Christmas Book*. (See bibliography on page 70.) Give the birds a wintertime treat by making a special tree for them. Tie a piece of yarn on a pinecone. Roll the pinecone in peanut butter and then in birdseed. Hang the pinecone on a tree. You may also use stale doughnuts and press in sunflower seeds. Use a yarn string and tie the doughnuts to a tree.

Snow Globes

In Jane Hissey's *Jolly Snow*, the toy animals try to make their own snow after finding a snow globe. Use baby food jars, water-resistant contact cement, and a plastic ornament to make snow globes. Glue the ornament to the inside of the lid. Fill the baby food jar with distilled water. A turkey baster is ideal for adding the water. Add a teaspoon of glitter. Place a thin layer of glue around the top edge of the baby food jar. Screw the top on and allow the glue to dry overnight. Turn the snow globe over and shake up a glittering snowstorm.

MUSIC/GAME EXPERIENCE

Christmas Caroling

Read "Singing Christmas Carols" in Jack Prelutsky's *It's Christmas* and *What a Morning! The Christmas Story in Black Spirituals* by John Langstaff. (See bibliography on this page.) Learn Christmas songs and go to other classrooms to sing for friends.

Din Dan Don

Din Dan Don It's Christmas by Janina Domanska is the text of a Polish Christmas carol. (See bibliography on this page.) Ask each child to choose an animal to represent and act out the different parts with rhythm instruments. Have a narrator read the story.

Sugar Plum Fairy

Read *The Story of the Nutcracker Ballet* by Deborah Hautzig. (See bibliography on this page.) Use the Christmas stars from figure 4.9 and move to the music "Sugar Plum Fairy" by Pamela Copus and Joyce Harlow in *Holiday Story Play Music*. (See bibliography on page 70.)

BIBLIOGRAPHY

Ahlberg, Janet, and Allan Ahlberg. *The Jolly Christmas Postman*. Boston: Little, Brown, 1991.

Andersen, Hans Christian. *The Fir Tree*. New York: Harper & Row, 1970.

Brett, Jan. *The Wild Christmas Reindeer*. New York: Scholastic, 1990.

Brown, Margaret Wise. *On Christmas Eve*. Reading, MA: Addison Wesley, 1938.

Carlstrom, Nancy White. *The Snow Speaks*. Boston: Little, Brown, 1992.

Climo, Shirley. *The Cobweb Christmas*. New York: Harper & Row, 1982.

Counihan, Claire. *The Twelve Days of Christmas*. New York: Scholastic, 1989.

Domanska, Janina. *Din Dan Don It's Christmas*. New York: Greenwillow Books, 1975.

Galdone, Paul. *The Elves and the Shoemaker*. New York: Clarion Books, 1984.

Greene, Ellin. *The Legend of the Christmas Rose*. New York: Holiday House, 1990.

Hautzig, Deborah. *The Story of the Nutcracker Ballet*. New York: Random House, 1983.

Hissey, Jane. *Jolly Snow*. New York: Philomel Books, 1991.

Langstaff, John. *What a Morning! The Christmas Story in Black Spirituals*. New York: Macmillan, 1987.

Littledale, Freya. *The Elves and the Shoemaker*. New York: Scholastic, 1975.

Plume, Ilse. *The Shoemaker and the Elves*. San Diego, CA: Harcourt Brace Jovanovich, 1991.

Polacco, Patricia. *Uncle Vova's Tree*. New York: Philomel Books, 1989.

Prelutsky, Jack. *It's Christmas*. New York: Greenwillow Books, 1981.

Pushker, Gloria Teles. *Toby Belfer Never Had a Christmas Tree*. Gretna, LA: Pelican, 1991.

Taylor, Jane. *Twinkle, Twinkle, Little Star*. New York: Scholastic, 1992.

Tudor, Tasha. *Take Joy! The Tasha Tudor Christmas Book*. Cleveland, OH: World, 1966.

Watts, Bernadette. *The Elves and the Shoemaker*. New York: Henry Holt, 1986.

Wells, Carolyn. *A Christmas Alphabet*. New York: G. P. Putnam's Sons, 1989.

Music

Copus, Pamela, and Joyce Harlow. "Sugar Plum Fairy." *Holiday Story Play Music*. Plano, TX: Dreamtime Productions, P.O. Box 940061, Plano, TX 75094-0061.

CHINESE NEW YEAR

DRAMA/PLAY EXPERIENCE

Read *Why Rat Comes First: A Story of the Chinese Zodiac* by Clara Yen to introduce the theme of Chinese New Year. (See bibliography on page 89.) *Why Rat Comes First* is a lively account of why the rat is the first symbol in the Chinese zodiac. Demonstrate the simpletees costumes and play props.

Simpletees Costumes

Use the simpletees costumes of the Jade King, the rat, and the ox for a dramatic play experience. (See figure 5.1.)

Play Props

Play props can include plastic oranges, apples, bowls, chopsticks, and a tablecloth for a New Year's feast.

Face Masks

Create face masks of the Jade King, the rat, and the ox. Use tagboard templates and trace the different characters. (See figures 5.2, 5.3, and 5.4.)

Stick Puppets/Paper Bag Theater

Make stick puppets of the Jade King, the rat, and the ox. (See figure 5.5.) Create a paper bag theater for the stick puppets. (See figure 1.5 on page 6.) Present the story of the Jade King, the rat, and the ox to a friend or take home to present to families.

(Text continues on page 77.)

Fig. 5.1. Simpletees costumes: Chinese New Year.

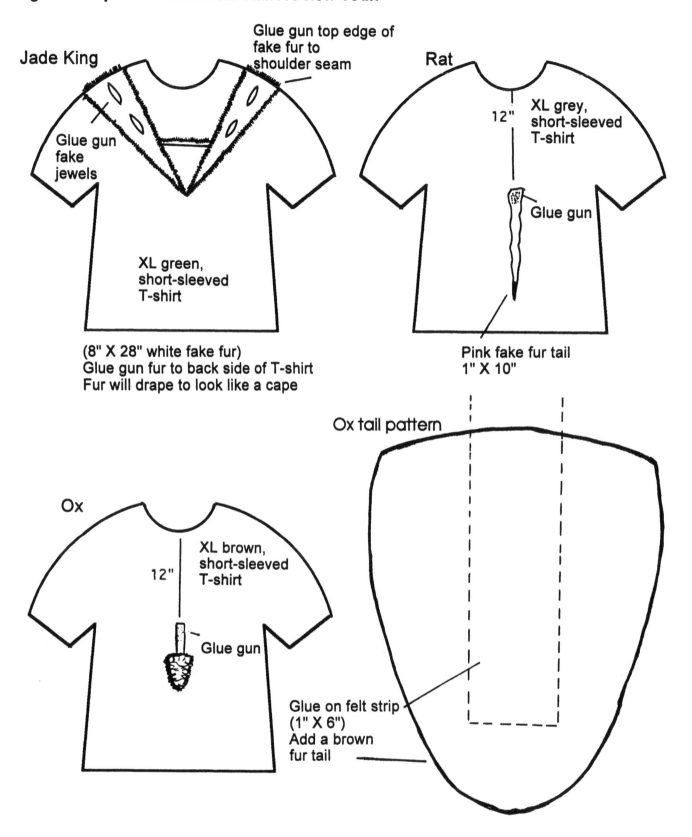

Jade King

Glue gun top edge of
fake fur to
shoulder seam

Glue gun
fake
jewels

XL green,
short-sleeved
T-shirt

(8" X 28" white fake fur)
Glue gun fur to back side of T-shirt
Fur will drape to look like a cape

Rat

12"

XL grey,
short-sleeved
T-shirt

Glue gun

Pink fake fur tail
1" X 10"

Ox tail pattern

Ox

12"

XL brown,
short-sleeved
T-shirt

Glue gun

Glue on felt strip
(1" X 6")
Add a brown
fur tail

Fig. 5.2. Jade King face mask pattern.

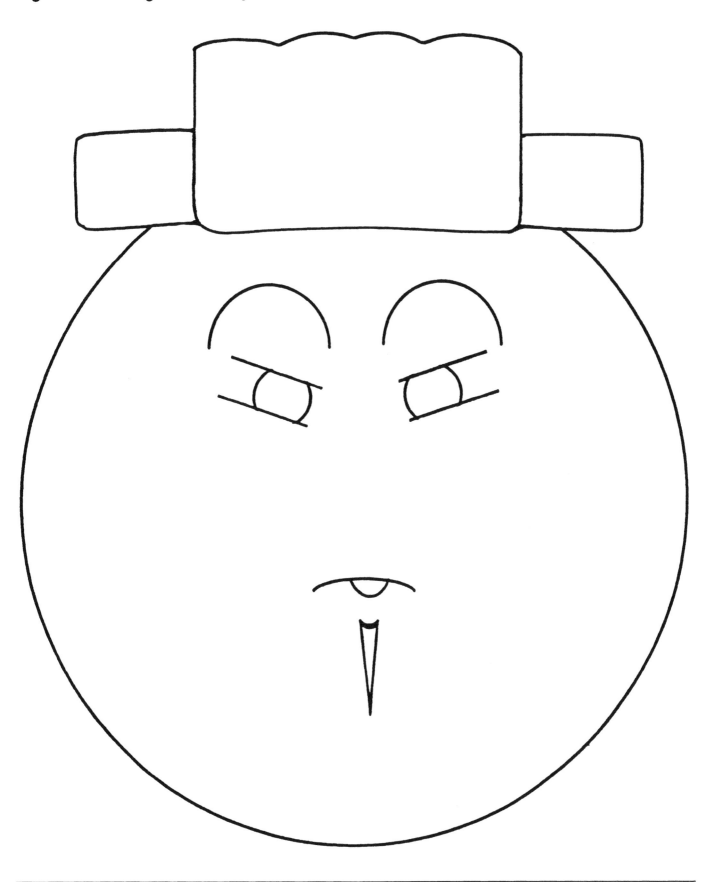

Fig. 5.3. Rat face mask pattern.

Fig. 5.4. Ox face mask pattern.

Fig. 5.5. Chinese New Year stick puppet patterns.

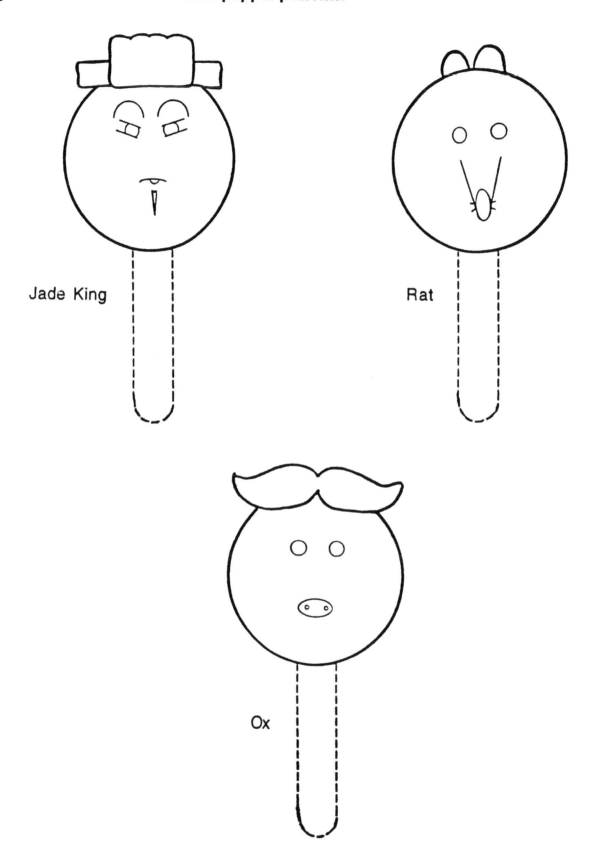

Jade King

Rat

Ox

LITERATURE/WRITING EXPERIENCE

Chinese New Year *Versions*

Sample a variety of books about Chinese New Year. For example, *Chinese New Year* by Tricia Brown and *Gung Hay Fat Choy* by June Behrens provide photographic accounts of Chinese New Year celebrations. Kate Waters and Madeline Slovenz-Low's *Lion Dancer: Ernie Wan's Chinese New Year* is another photographic account that takes the reader through a little boy's Chinese New Year activities. *Mei Li* by Thomas Handforth is the classic story of a little Chinese girl who sneaks off to go to a New Year's fair. (See bibliography on page 89.)

Chinese New Year *Children's Version*

Write a children's version about Chinese New Year on a large sheet of chart paper.

Key-Word Books and Key Words

Make a key-word book with the unique or important words from *Why Rat Comes First: A Story of the Chinese Zodiac* by Clara Yen. (See bibliography on page 89.) The key words for *Why Rat Comes First* are as follows:

Jade King	rat	ox
animals	big	small
year	feast	twelve
invitation		

Fan Shape Book

Make a fan shape book by tracing the fan shape from a tagboard template. (See figure 5.6.) Illustrate the book and write a story or dictate it to the teacher. Use the key words for an independent writing experience.

Fig. 5.6. Fan shape book directions and pattern.

Materials:

Red construction paper
Tagboard
White paper
Scissors
Stapler
Markers or pencils
Key words

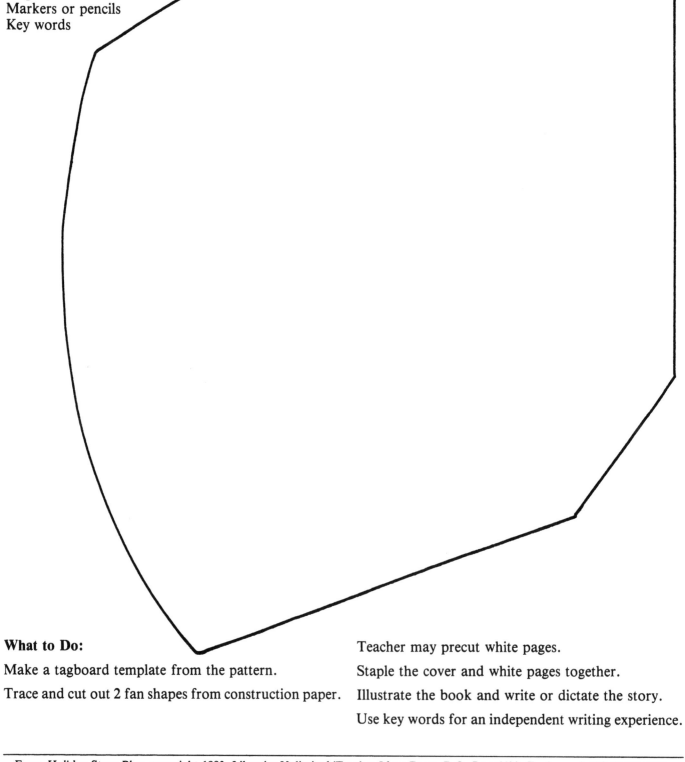

What to Do:

Make a tagboard template from the pattern.

Trace and cut out 2 fan shapes from construction paper.

Teacher may precut white pages.

Staple the cover and white pages together.

Illustrate the book and write or dictate the story.

Use key words for an independent writing experience.

COOPERATIVE/GROUP EXPERIENCE

Feast of Lanterns

Read *The Chinese New Year* by Cheng Hou-tien, which gives a detailed account of the preparation and celebration of this important Chinese festival. Make a lantern for a class Chinese New Year parade. (See figure 5.7.) Carry the lanterns and go on a parade inside or outside.

Fig. 5.7. Chinese lantern directions and illustration.

Materials:

Construction paper (9" X 12")
Masking tape
Scissors
Stapler

What to Do:

Place a strip of masking tape along the 12" sides of the construction paper.

Fold the paper in half lengthwise with the masking tape sides face up.

Cut 1" strips from the fold to the masking tape.

Open and staple the 9" sides together to form a cylinder.

Attach a paper handle to the top.

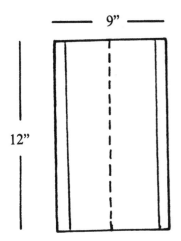 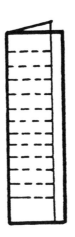 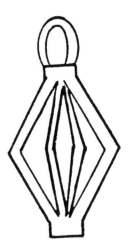

Dragon Trap

Henry and the Dragon by Eileen Christelow is the delightful story of a small rabbit's attempt to trap a dragon. (See bibliography on page 89.) Build a dragon trap in the classroom by using crepe paper and weaving it throughout the furniture and fixtures. Use a fortune cookie as bait to catch a dragon.

Jade King Feast

In *Why Rat Comes First: A Story of the Chinese Zodiac* by Clara Yen, the Jade King invites the animals to a feast. (See bibliography on page 89.) Select an animal from the Chinese zodiac and write an invitation to that animal to come to a feast.

Wishing Tree

Read Jeanne M. Lee's *The Legend of the Milky Way*, a retelling of an old Chinese legend about a shepherd and a weaver princess who fall in love but are allowed to be together only once a year. (See bibliography on page 89.) Make a wishing tree by writing or illustrating a wish on a piece of paper. Tie the wishes to a real tree.

Dragon Descriptions

In Jay Williams's *Everyone Knows What a Dragon Looks Like*, a small, fat, bald, old man turns into a beautiful but frightening dragon. (See bibliography on page 89.) Using a large sheet of paper, each child illustrates a part of the dragon to create one big dragon. Write or dictate descriptions of the dragon and draw word balloons around the descriptions. For example, "It looks like a green glob," and "It looks angry."

ART/CRAFT EXPERIENCE

Tempera Painting

Dragons Dragons & Other Creatures That Never Were by Eric Carle is illustrated with dragons and other mythological creatures. (See bibliography on page 89.) Create dragons by using green, purple, and red tempera paint. Write a caption for each dragon painting. Display the paintings on the wall or the bulletin board. Bind the paintings together to make a class book.

Paper-Plate Dragon

The Dragon's Robe by Deborah Nourse Lattimore retells a Chinese tale in which a young girl named Kwan Yin weaves a robe for the rain dragon and thereby saves the land. (See bibliography on page 89.) Make a paper-plate dragon to illustrate the story. (See figure 5.8.)

Dragon Kite

In *Dragon Kite of the Autumn Moon* by Valerie Reddix, a young boy faces a dilemma about cutting the string on the treasured dragon kite made by his ailing grandmother. (See bibliography on page 89.) Make a dragon kite. (See figure 5.9.) Fly the kite outdoors as part of a Chinese New Year celebration.

(Text continues on page 83.)

Fig. 5.8. Paper-plate dragon directions and illustration.

Materials:

Paper plates
Paint or markers
Paper streamers
Brads
Craft sticks

What to Do:

Each child decorates a paper plate with paint or markers.

Add paper streamers.

Connect plates together with brads.

Attach craft sticks to carry the dragon and to make it move.

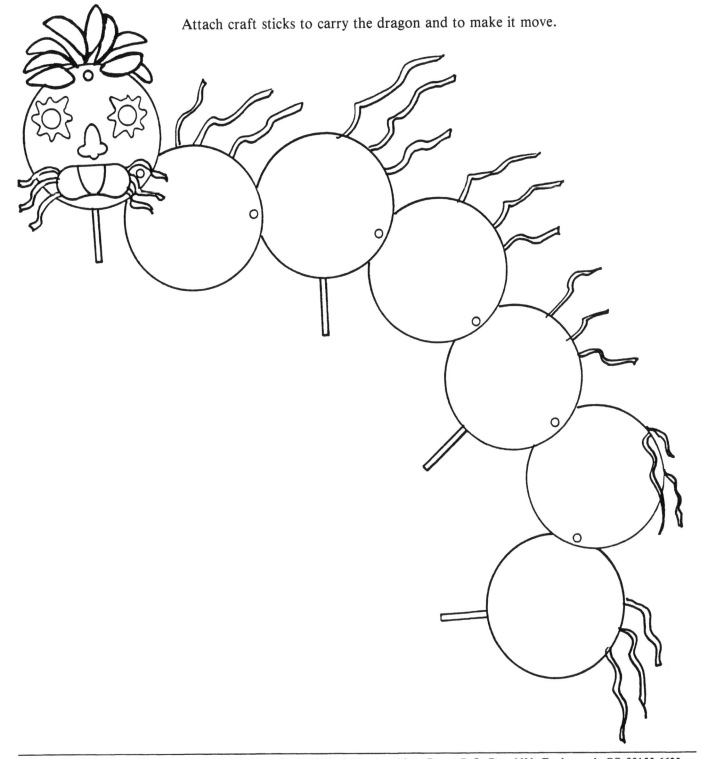

Fig. 5.9. Dragon kite directions and illustration.

Materials:

18" X 24" white art paper
Stapler
Shredded paper
Markers or crayons
Hole punch
Kite string
Glue
Art tissue

What to Do:

Fold paper in half.

Fold in half again and staple a 1" edge along the bottom and side to make a pocket.

Stuff with shredded paper.

Fold down top edge and staple together.

Punch two holes in top edge.

Insert and tie a 24" kite string through the holes to form a V shape.

Tie another string, approximately 24" long, to the V-shape string.

Draw a dragon face on the kite.

Glue tissue streamers to the bottom edge.

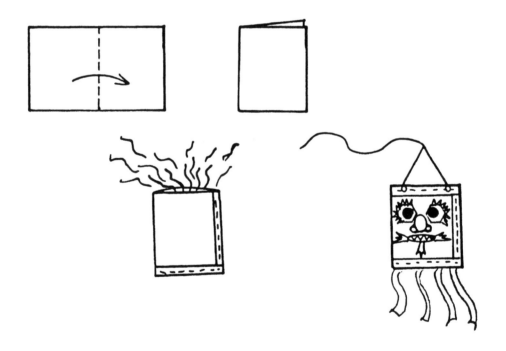

From *Holiday Story Play*, copyright 1993. Libraries Unlimited/Teacher Ideas Press, P.O. Box 6633, Englewood, CO 80155-6633.

COOKING/MATH EXPERIENCE

Fortune Cookies

Make your very own fortune cookies to celebrate Chinese New Year. Purchase a can of flaky biscuits and follow the recipe in figure 5.10.

Dumplings

How the Ox Star Fell from Heaven by Lily Toy Hong tells the Chinese legend of how the Ox Star made it possible for people to grow enough food to keep from going hungry. (See bibliography on page 89.) Make dumplings from flaky biscuits and chicken broth. Separate the biscuit layers and cut into fourths. Dip the biscuit bits into boiling chicken broth and cook for approximately 10 minutes. Use chopsticks to eat the dumplings.

Chinese Number Snacks

Read *Count Your Way Through China* by Jim Haskins. This unique book describes many aspects of Chinese culture while teaching the reader to count to 10 in Chinese. (See bibliography on page 89.) Prepare Chinese number cards and use them at the snack center to count out the amount of snack to eat. (See figure 5.11.)

Tangrams

Grandfather Tang's Story by Ann Tompert and *The Tangram Magician* by Lisa Campbell Ernst and Lee Ernst are two excellent stories to introduce the use of tangrams. (See bibliography on page 89.) Make a set of tangrams to use while reading these stories. (See figure 5.12.)

(Text continues on page 87.)

Fig. 5.10. Fortune cookie recipe.

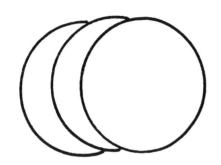

separate
flaky biscuits

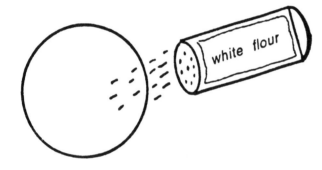

shake on flour

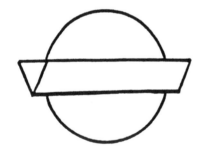

insert message

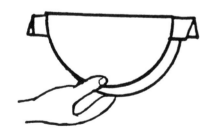

fold up and
pinch together
bake at 425⁰ for 10
minutes
(remove message before eating)

Fig. 5.11. Chinese number cards.

1 / 一 / **yee**   2 / 二 / **uhr**

3 / 三 / **sahn**   4 / 四 / **suh**

5 / 五 / **woo**   6 / 六 / **lyo**

7 / 七 / **chee**   8 / 八 / **bah**

9 / 九 / **jo**   10 / 十 / **shur**

Fig. 5.12. Tangram pattern and directions.

Materials:

Red copy or construction paper
Scissors
Envelope

What to Do:

Copy pattern on the red paper.

Cut pieces apart along the lines.

Place the pieces in the envelope.

Make figures by rearranging the tangram pieces.

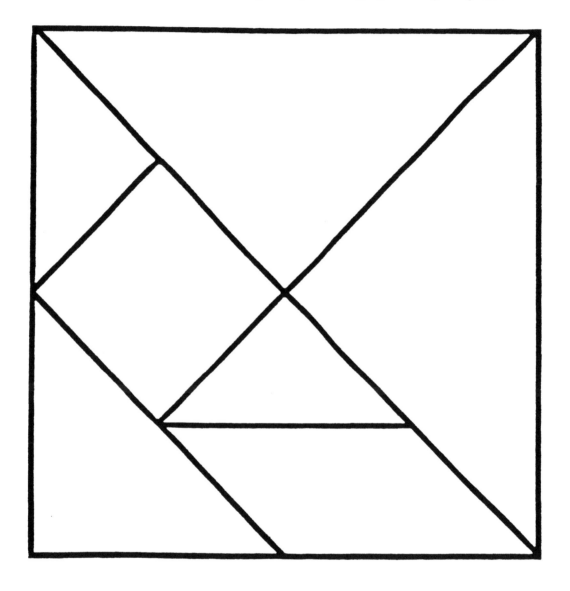

SCIENCE/DISCOVERY EXPERIENCE

Discovery Museum

Create a discovery museum to display items and books about China. Have the children contribute a variety of items from China, such as chopsticks, fans, kites, flags, and other collectables. Display the items on a table, shelf, or counter top in the classroom. Use sentence strips to label the items. Explore the museum with the group or individually.

Popcorn Dragons

Read Jane Thayer's *The Popcorn Dragon*, in which a little dragon learns that he can make popcorn by breathing on ears of corn. (See bibliography on page 89.) If the day is cold enough, go outside and watch your "dragon" breath form in the cold air. Warm up inside by popping popcorn for snack time.

Snapdragons

In *Harriet and William and the Terrible Creature* by Valerie Scho Carey, twins Harriet and William help out a lonely dragon in outer space by showing him how to grow a flower garden. (See bibliography on page 89.) Plant snapdragons in a clear plastic cup filled with dirt. Watch the snapdragons grow and record the daily observations on a class chart.

MUSIC/GAME EXPERIENCE

Dance of the Lions

In *Lion Dancer: Ernie Wan's Chinese New Year* by Kate Waters and Madeline Slovenz-Low, Ernie participates in his first lion dance. (See bibliography on page 89.) Celebrate Chinese New Year by performing a lion dance. Make a lion mask. (See figure 5.13.) Listen to "Dance of the Lions" by Pamela Copus and Joyce Harlow in *Holiday Story Play Music* or use traditional Chinese music. (See bibliography on page 89.)

Dragon's Tail

In China, the dragon is the symbol of strength and wisdom. It is also believed to keep evil spirits away from the New Year celebration. Play the dragon tail game by forming a line. Place hands on the shoulders of the person in front. The dragon's head is the first person in line, the tail is the last person in line. On the count of three, the head attempts to catch the tail without breaking the line. The dragon's body will break if anyone lets go of the shoulders in front.

Chinese Mother Goose Rhymes

Read *Chinese Mother Goose Rhymes* by Robert Wyndham. (See bibliography on page 89.) Experience the rhyme about the dragon:

As the sun came up, a ball of red,

I followed my friend wherever he led.

He thought his fast horse would leave me behind,

But I rode a dragon as swift as the wind!

Fig. 5.13. Lion mask directions and illustration.

Materials:	**What to Do:**
Brown grocery bag	Cut 4" slits around the bottom of the bag and cut out eye holes.
Scissors	
Markers and pencils	Curl lion mane around a pencil.
Shredded paper	
Glue	Use markers and draw the features.
	Glue shredded paper on the top of the bag.

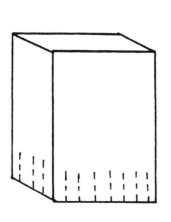
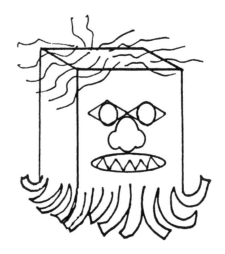

BIBLIOGRAPHY

Behrens, June. *Gung Hay Fat Choy*. Chicago: Children's Press, 1982.

Brown, Tricia. *Chinese New Year*. New York: Henry Holt, 1987.

Carey, Valerie Scho. *Harriet and William and the Terrible Creature*. New York: Dutton Children's Books, 1985.

Carle, Eric. *Dragons Dragons & Other Creatures That Never Were*. New York: Philomel Books, 1991.

Christelow, Eileen. *Henry and the Dragon*. New York: Clarion Books, 1984.

Ernst, Lisa Campbell, and Lee Ernst. *The Tangram Magician*. New York: Harry N. Abrams, 1990.

Handforth, Thomas. *Mei Li*. New York: Doubleday, 1938.

Haskins, Jim. *Count Your Way Through China*. Minneapolis, MN: Carolrhoda Books, 1987.

Hong, Lily Toy. *How the Ox Star Fell from Heaven*. Morton Grove, IL: Albert Whitman, 1991.

Hou-tien, Cheng. *The Chinese New Year*. New York: Holt, Rinehart & Winston, 1976.

Lattimore, Deborah Nourse. *The Dragon's Robe*. New York: Harper & Row, 1990.

Lee, Jeanne M. *The Legend of the Milky Way*. New York: Henry Holt, 1982.

Reddix, Valerie. *Dragon Kite of the Autumn Moon*. New York: Lothrop, Lee & Shepard, 1991.

Thayer, Jane. *The Popcorn Dragon*. New York: Scholastic, 1953.

Tompert, Ann. *Grandfather Tang's Story*. New York: Crown, 1990.

Waters, Kate, and Madeline Slovenz-Low. *Lion Dancer: Ernie Wan's Chinese New Year*. New York: Scholastic, 1990.

Williams, Jay. *Everyone Knows What a Dragon Looks Like*. New York: Aladdin Books, 1976.

Wyndham, Robert. *Chinese Mother Goose Rhymes*. New York: Philomel Books, 1968.

Yen, Clara. *Why Rat Comes First: A Story of the Chinese Zodiac*. San Francisco: Children's Book Press, 1991.

Music

Copus, Pamela, and Joyce Harlow. "Dance of the Lions." *Holiday Story Play Music*. Plano, TX: Dreamtime Productions, P.O. Box 940061, Plano, TX 75094-0061.

VALENTINE'S DAY

DRAMA/PLAY EXPERIENCE

Read the traditional nursery rhyme "The Queen of Hearts" in *Tomie dePaola's Mother Goose* and *The Missing Tarts* by B. G. Hennessy to introduce the theme of Valentine's Day. (See bibliography on page 104.) In *The Missing Tarts*, the Queen of Hearts's tarts have disappeared and the other nursery rhyme characters advise her on where to find them. Demonstrate the simpletees costumes and play props.

Simpletees Costumes

Use the simpletees costumes of the Queen of Hearts, the King of Hearts, and the Knave of Hearts for a dramatic play experience. (See figures 6.1 and 6.2.)

Play Props

Play props can include a mixing bowl, a wooden spoon, a cookie tray, a rolling pin, and a variety of heart-shaped objects.

Face Masks

Create face masks of the Queen of Hearts, the King of Hearts, and the Knave of Hearts. Use tagboard templates and trace the different characters. (See figures 6.3, 6.4, and 6.5.)

Stick Puppets/Paper Bag Theater

Make stick puppets of the Queen of Hearts, the King of Hearts, and the Knave of Hearts. (See figure 6.6.) Create a paper bag theater for the stick puppets. (See figure 1.5 on page 6.) Present the story of the missing tarts to a friend or take home and present to parents.

(Text continues on page 97.)

Fig. 6.1. Simpletees costumes: Valentine's Day.

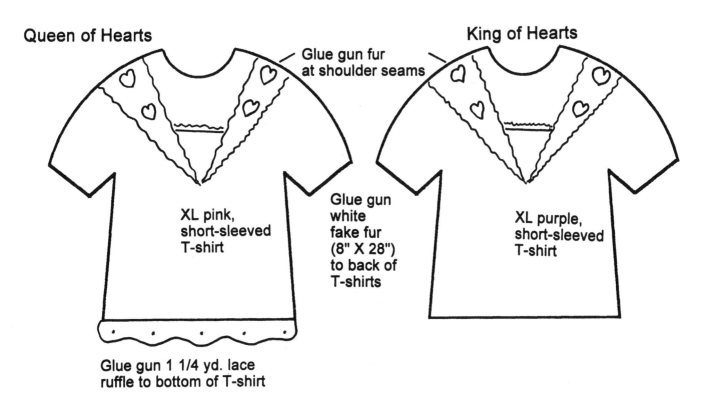

Queen of Hearts

King of Hearts

Glue gun fur
at shoulder seams

XL pink,
short-sleeved
T-shirt

Glue gun
white
fake fur
(8" X 28")
to back of
T-shirts

XL purple,
short-sleeved
T-shirt

Glue gun 1 1/4 yd. lace
ruffle to bottom of T-shirt

Knave of Hearts

XL red,
short-sleeved
T-shirt

Fig. 6.2. Knave of Hearts tunic directions.

Materials:

12" X 32" pink felt
Scissors
Glue gun

What to Do:

Fold felt in half lengthwise.

Cut out the neck opening and the heart shapes.

Glue gun the pink felt tunic to an XL red, short-sleeved T-shirt at the neck opening.

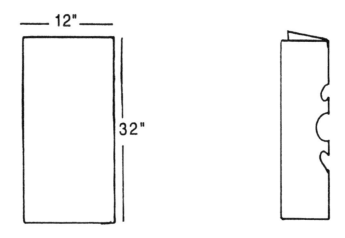

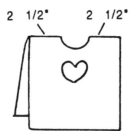

Fig. 6.3. Queen of Hearts face mask pattern.

Fig. 6.4. King of Hearts face mask pattern.

Fig. 6.5. Knave of Hearts face mask pattern.

Fig. 6.6. Valentine's Day stick puppet patterns.

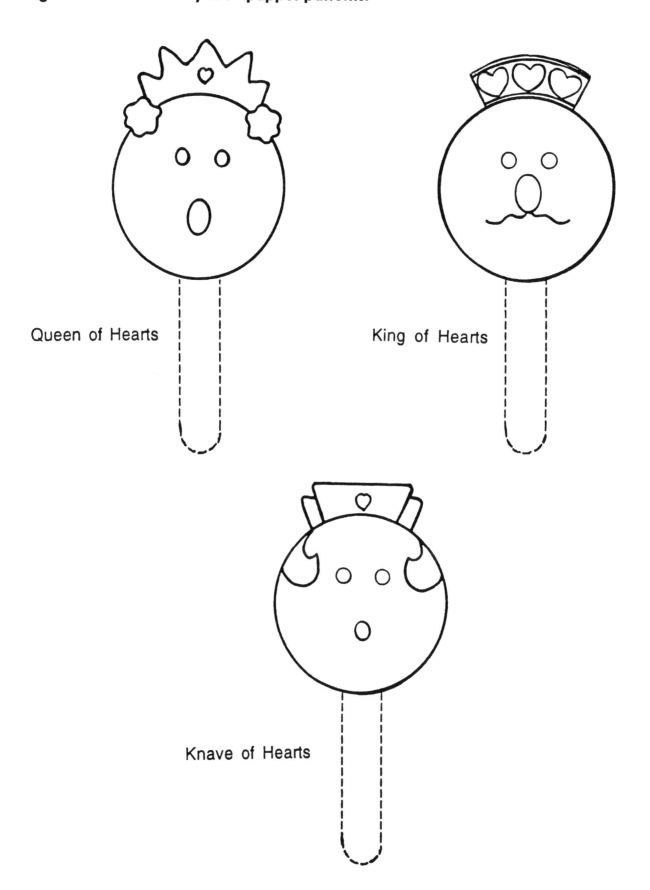

Queen of Hearts

King of Hearts

Knave of Hearts

LITERATURE/WRITING EXPERIENCE

Valentine's Day *Versions*

Experience a variety of stories about Valentine's Day. For example, *Valentine's Day* by Gail Gibbons and Joyce K. Kessel's *Valentine's Day* tell how the current customs surrounding Valentine's Day came about. *Valentine's Day* by Miriam Nerlove gives a brief history of Valentine's Day while telling how a little girl celebrates the day. Margery Cuyler's *Freckles and Willie* offers a different perspective on the meaning of Valentine's Day, and Lorna Balian's *A Sweetheart for Valentine* offers a unique reason for celebrating on February 14. (See bibliography on page 104.)

Valentine's Day *Children's Version*

Write a children's version about Valentine's Day on a large sheet of chart paper.

Key-Word Books and Key Words

Make a key-word book with the unique or important words from Tomie dePaola's "The Queen of Hearts" and *The Missing Tarts* by B. G. Hennessy. (See bibliography on page 104.) The key words for "The Queen of Hearts" and *The Missing Tarts* are as follows:

Queen	Knave	King
Hearts	stole	steal
tarts	kiss	Valentine's Day

Heart Shape Book

Make a heart shape book by tracing the heart shape from a tagboard template. (See figure 6.7.) Illustrate the book and write a story or dictate it to the teacher. Use the key words for an independent writing experience.

Valentine Postal Center

Read *The Jolly Postman* by Janet Ahlberg and Allan Ahlberg and Gail Gibbons's *The Post Office Book: Mail and How It Moves.* (See bibliography on page 104.) Set up a classroom post office. Use cardboard boxes with dividers, such as empty liquor boxes (be sure to decorate so that brand names are covered). Label the compartments with the children's names. Write letters and valentines to friends and place in small envelopes. Deliver the letters and valentines to the proper mail slots.

Fig. 6.7. Heart shape book directions and pattern.

Materials:

Red construction paper
Tagboard
White paper
Scissors
Stapler
Markers or pencils
Key words

What to Do:

Make a tagboard template from the pattern.

Trace and cut out 2 heart shapes from construction paper.

Teacher may precut white pages.

Staple the cover and white pages together.

Illustrate the book and write or dictate the story.

Use key words for an independent writing experience.

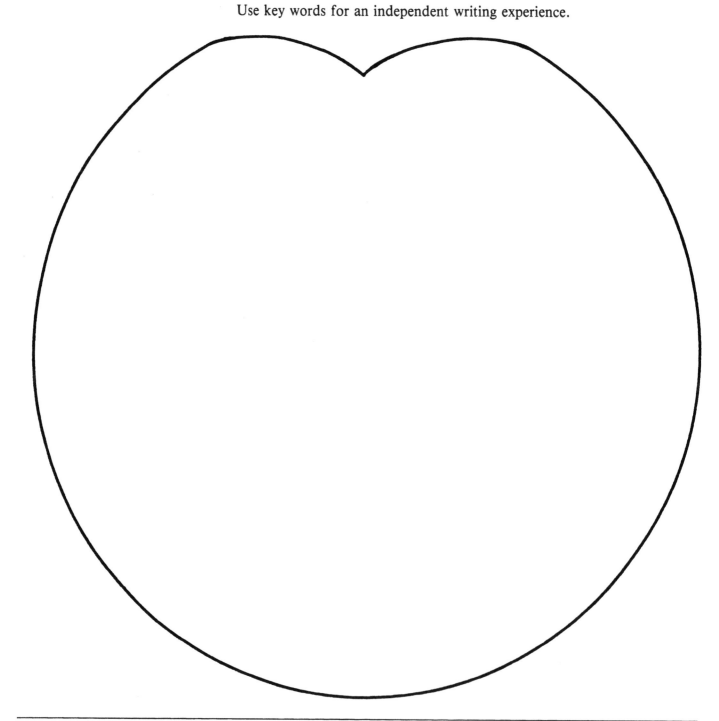

The Dove's Letter

A dove decides to give a beautiful letter a very special delivery in *The Dove's Letter* by Keith Baker. (See bibliography on page 104.) Each recipient finds a different meaning for the message inside. Make a special letter similar to the dove's. (See figure 6.8.)

Messages in a Tube

Read *Messages in the Mailbox: How to Write a Letter* by Loreen Leedy. (See bibliography on page 104.) Write a message and put it in a paper tube. Use tissue paper and wrap the tube. Use ribbon or yarn to tie the ends. Give the message to a parent, guardian, or friend.

Fig. 6.8. Dove's letter directions and illustration.

Materials:

Blue or pink 9" X 12" construction
    paper
Ribbon, lace, or paper strip
Scissors
Glue
Markers or pencils

What to Do:

Cut construction paper in half (4½" X 12").

Cut a ribbon, lace, or paper strip 1" X 12".

Fold construction paper in thirds.

Cut slits at each end of the paper and weave the ribbon, lace, or paper strip through them.

Glue or staple strips in place.

Fold down the ribbon and the corners of the top section of the construction paper to form an envelope flap.

Write a message in the center section.

Give the letter to a special valentine.

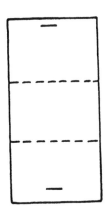

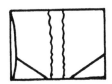

Heart Puzzle

Read *Somebody Loves You, Mr. Hatch* by Eileen Spinelli. (See bibliography on page 104.) After Mr. Hatch receives a mysterious package on Valentine's Day, his life will never be the same again. Make a heart-shaped puzzle by cutting a heart out of construction paper. Write a message on the heart. Cut the heart into four or five pieces and place them in an envelope. Give the puzzle to somebody you love on Valentine's Day.

COOPERATIVE/GROUP EXPERIENCE

Where's Cupid?

A favorite symbol of Valentine's Day is Cupid. Read *Where's Cupid?* by Anthony Tallarico and find Cupid as he shoots his arrow at the unsuspecting couples on each page. (See bibliography on page 104.) Make a mural to hide cupids in. Use red, pink, and purple tempera and paint a mural of hearts and flowers. Be sure to fill the entire paper. Allow the paper to dry and then hide tiny Cupids in the painting. Post a sentence strip with the title "Where's Cupid?"

More than Applesauce

Read "I Love You More Than Applesauce" in *It's Valentine's Day* by Jack Prelutsky. (See bibliography on page 104.) Use a large heart cutout and let each child supply an answer to "I love you more than _____." Write the responses inside the hearts.

ART/CRAFT EXPERIENCE

Tempera Painting

Read *The Missing Tarts* by B. G. Hennessy, a retelling of the traditional nursery rhyme "The Queen of Hearts." (See bibliography on page 104.) Use pink, red, purple, yellow, peach, and brown tempera paint to paint a picture of the Queen of Hearts. Write a caption for the painting. Display the paintings on the walls or the bulletin board. Bind the paintings together to make a class book.

Valentine Necklace

Read *Four Valentines in a Rainstorm* by Felicia Bond. (See bibliography on page 104.) When it started raining hearts, Cornelia Augusta caught enough to make valentines for her special friends. Use red and pink construction-paper hearts, drinking straws cut into one-inch pieces, and red or pink yarn to make a valentine necklace for your special valentine.

Scented Valentines

In Frank Modell's *One Zillion Valentines*, Marvin and Milton make a zillion valentines and learn that to get valentines you must give them. (See bibliography on page 104.) Make a fragrant valentine by mixing a package of raspberry-, strawberry-, or cherry-flavored gelatin with just enough water to form a paste. Use a paint brush to paint the paste in a heart shape on a piece of construction paper. Allow the valentine to dry overnight. Give the valentine to someone special. Perhaps you will receive a valentine in return.

Hearts' Garden

Listen to "Hearts' Garden" by Pamela Copus and Joyce Harlow. (See bibliography on page 104.) While listening to the music, paint a mural of a garden filled with hearts. Place a long sheet of mural paper on a table or attach the paper to a wall. Use red, pink, blue, and magenta tempera to make the hearts and add green tempera for the stems.

COOKING/MATH EXPERIENCE

Queen of Hearts' Tarts

Make Queen of Hearts tarts. Separate in half each biscuit from a can of flaky biscuits. Place one teaspoon of cherry pie filling on one half of the biscuit. Place the other biscuit half on top and crimp the edges together with a fork. Bake at 425 degrees for 10 to 13 minutes or until brown.

Peanuts in a Shell

Read the following poem from Alice Low's *The Family Read-Aloud Holiday Treasury*. (See bibliography on page 104.) Serve peanuts in the shell at snack time.

> I love you,
>
> I love you,
>
> I love you
>
> so well,
>
> If I had a peanut,
>
> I'd give you
>
> the shell.
>
> —Anonymous

Heart-Shaped Sandwiches

In *The Valentine Bears* by Eve Bunting, Mrs. Bear fixes a special Valentine's Day treat for Mr. Bear. (See bibliography on page 104.) Make heart-shaped sandwiches by following the recipe in figure 6.9. Soften cream cheese and tint it with red food coloring. Spread the cream cheese on a slice of white bread. Add a top slice of bread and cut it with a heart-shaped cookie cutter.

Fig. 6.9. Heart-shaped sandwich.

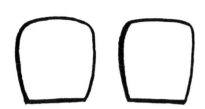

2 slices bread

cream cheese

spread pink cream cheese

make a sandwich

cut heart shape

SCIENCE/DISCOVERY EXPERIENCE

Discovery Museum

Create a discovery museum to display contributions, collections, and books about Valentine's Day. Display the items on a table, shelf, or counter top in the classroom. Use sentence strips to label the items. Explore the museum with a group or individually.

Invisible Ink Message

Read *The Mysterious Valentine* by Nancy Carlson and try to discover, along with Louanne, who could possibly have sent the most beautiful valentine she had ever seen. (See bibliography on page 104.) Use milk and cotton swabs to write a secret message on white paper. Allow it to dry. Place the paper between two pieces of scrap paper and have the teacher iron over the message to make it appear. Send the secret valentine to surprise someone special.

Puffy Hearts

Buttercup and Lucy plan a special Valentine's Day party, with plenty of hearts, in *Valentine Friends* by Ann Schweninger. (See bibliography on page 104.) Make puffy hearts for a special valentine. Combine ¼ cup flour, ¼ cup salt, and ¼ cup water. Divide the mixture in half and add red tempera to one half and pink tempera to the other half. Pour the mixture into squeeze bottles. Use the squeeze bottles and mixture to make heart shapes on heavy paper. The hearts will puff up as they harden.

MUSIC/GAME EXPERIENCE

Postman, Postman

Choose one child to be the postman. That child sits in a chair with his or her back to the class. Place a valentine under the chair and select another child to take the valentine. All the children then chant, "Postman, postman, who's got your mail?" The postman then guesses who took the valentine. The valentine holder then becomes the postman. The game continues until all children have had a turn.

Names in a Jar

In *Valentine's Day* by Joyce K. Kessel, the ancient Roman tradition of dropping names in a jar is discussed. (See bibliography on page 104.) Play a names-in-the-jar game by writing names on slips of paper and placing them in a jar. Draw a name for your valentine of the day. Be sure to be nice to this valentine for the entire day.

BIBLIOGRAPHY

Ahlberg, Janet, and Allan Ahlberg. *The Jolly Postman or Other People's Letters*. Boston: Little, Brown, 1986.

Baker, Keith. *The Dove's Letter*. San Diego, CA: Harcourt Brace Jovanovich, 1988.

Balian, Lorna. *A Sweetheart for Valentine*. Nashville, TN: Abingdon Press, 1979.

Bond, Felicia. *Four Valentines in a Rainstorm*. New York: Harper Trophy, 1983.

Bunting, Eve. *The Valentine Bears*. New York: Clarion Books, 1983.

Carlson, Nancy. *The Mysterious Valentine*. New York: Puffin Books, 1985.

Cuyler, Margery. *Freckles and Willie*. New York: Henry Holt, 1986.

dePaola, Tomie. *Tomie dePaola's Mother Goose*. New York: G. P. Putnam's Sons, 1985.

Gibbons, Gail. *The Post Office Book: Mail and How It Moves*. New York: Harper & Row, 1986.

_____. *Valentine's Day*. New York: Holiday House, 1986.

Hennessy, B. G. *The Missing Tarts*. New York: Scholastic, 1989.

Kessel, Joyce K. *Valentine's Day*. Minneapolis, MN: Carolrhoda Books, 1981.

Leedy, Loreen. *Messages in the Mailbox: How to Write a Letter*. New York: Holiday House, 1991.

Low, Alice. *The Family Read-Aloud Holiday Treasury*. Boston: Little, Brown, 1991.

Modell, Frank. *One Zillion Valentines*. New York: Mulberry Books, 1981.

Nerlove, Miriam. *Valentine's Day*. Morton Grove, IL: Albert Whitman, 1992.

Prelutsky, Jack. *It's Valentine's Day*. New York: Greenwillow Books, 1983.

Schweninger, Ann. *Valentine Friends*. New York: Scholastic, 1988.

Spinelli, Eileen. *Somebody Loves You, Mr. Hatch*. New York: Bradbury Press, 1991.

Tallarico, Anthony. *Where's Cupid?* Chicago: Kidsbooks, 1992.

Music

Copus, Pamela, and Joyce Harlow. "Hearts' Garden." *Holiday Story Play Music*. Plano, TX: Dreamtime Productions, P.O. Box 940061, Plano, TX 75094-0061.

CHAPTER
7

ST. PATRICK'S DAY

DRAMA/PLAY EXPERIENCE

Read *Jamie O'Rourke and the Big Potato* by Tomie dePaola to introduce the theme of St. Patrick's Day. (See bibliography on page 118.) Jamie O'Rourke is a lazy Irishman who leaves all the work to his wife Eileen. When a leprechaun comes along, Jamie, Eileen, and the entire village are never the same again.

Simpletees Costumes

Use the simpletees costumes of Jamie, Eileen, and the leprechaun for a dramatic play experience. (See figure 7.1.)

Play Props

Play props can include plastic potatoes, a black plastic kettle, "gold pieces" (foil-covered candy or cardboard), a small apron, a sleep cap, and a pair of house slippers.

Face Masks

Create face masks of Jamie, Eileen, and the leprechaun. Use templates and trace the different characters. (See figures 7.2, 7.3, and 7.4.)

Stick Puppets/Paper Bag Theater

Make stick puppets of Jamie, Eileen, and the leprechaun. (See figure 7.5.) Create a paper bag theater for the stick puppets. (See figure 1.5 on page 6.) Present the story of Jamie, Eileen, and the leprechaun to a friend to take home and present to family.

(Text continues on page 111.)

Fig. 7.1. Simpletees costumes: St. Patrick's Day.

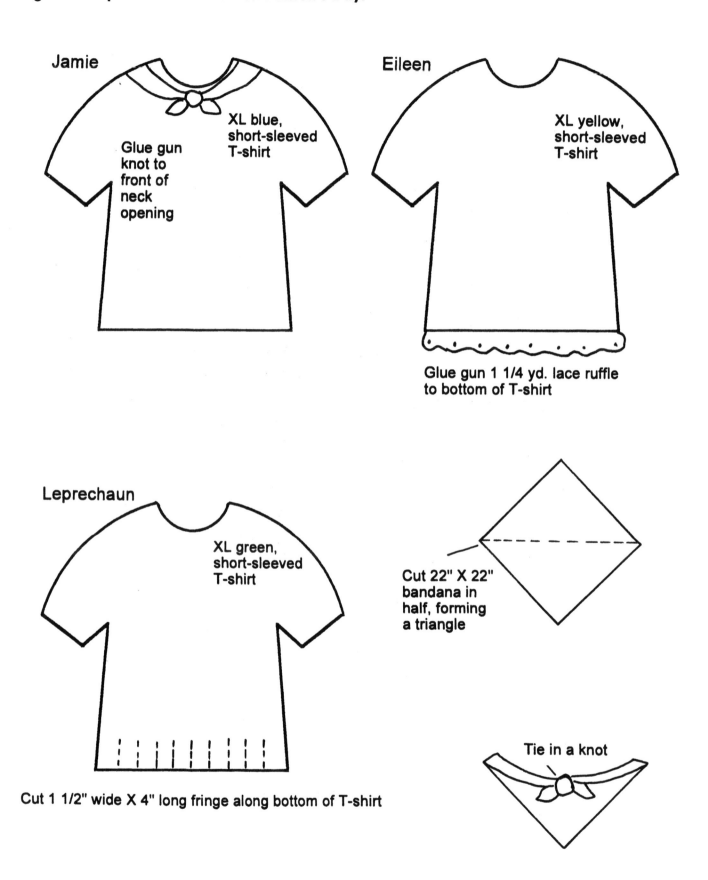

Jamie

XL blue, short-sleeved T-shirt

Glue gun knot to front of neck opening

Eileen

XL yellow, short-sleeved T-shirt

Glue gun 1 1/4 yd. lace ruffle to bottom of T-shirt

Leprechaun

XL green, short-sleeved T-shirt

Cut 1 1/2" wide X 4" long fringe along bottom of T-shirt

Cut 22" X 22" bandana in half, forming a triangle

Tie in a knot

Fig. 7.2. Jamie O'Rourke face mask pattern.

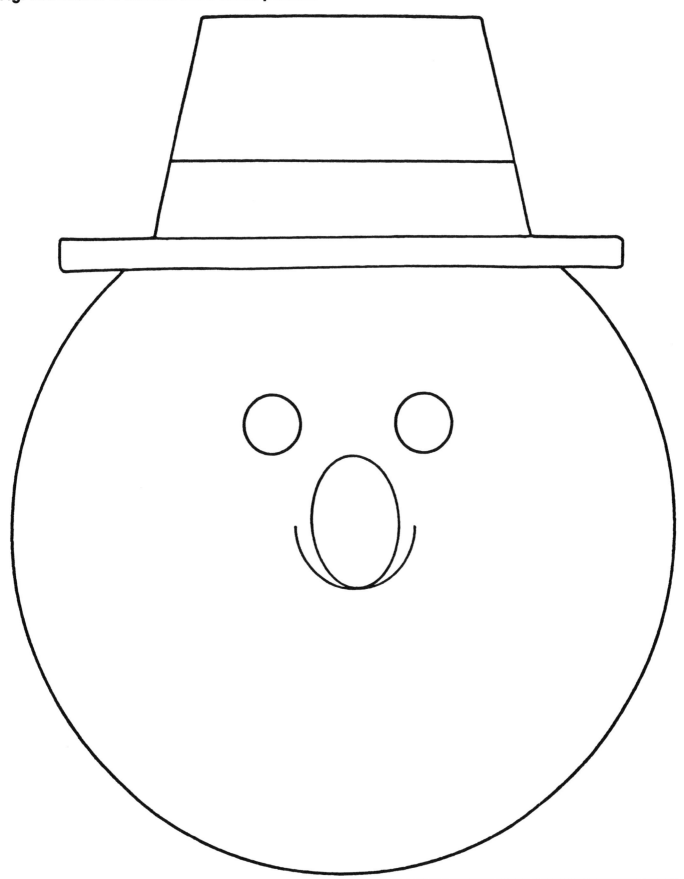

Fig. 7.3. Eileen face mask pattern.

Fig. 7.4. Leprechaun face mask pattern.

Fig. 7.5. St. Patrick's Day stick puppet patterns.

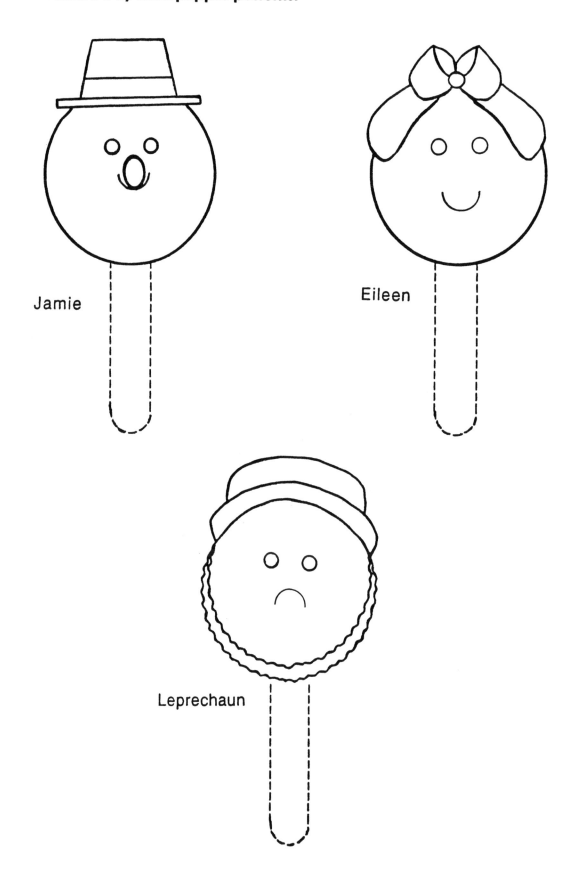

Jamie

Eileen

Leprechaun

LITERATURE/WRITING EXPERIENCE

St. Patrick's Day *Versions*

Experience a variety of stories about St. Patrick's Day. *St. Patrick's Day* by Joyce K. Kessel and *Shamrocks, Harps, and Shillelaghs* by Edna Barth answer many questions about the meaning of St. Patrick's Day and the traditions behind the celebration. (See bibliography on page 118.)

St. Patrick's Day *Children's Version*

Read Eve Bunting's *St. Patrick's Day in the Morning.* A little boy creates his own St. Patrick's Day parade. Recall your own past St. Patrick's Day celebrations. Now write a children's version about St. Patrick's Day on a large sheet of chart paper.

Key-Word Books and Key Words

Make a key-word book with the unique or important words from *Jamie O'Rourke and the Big Potato* by Tomie dePaola. (See bibliography on page 118.) The key words for *Jamie O'Rourke and the Big Potato* are as follows:

Jamie	Eileen	leprechaun
Ireland	potato	praties
lazy	wish	pot
gold		

Potato Shape Book

Make a potato shape book by tracing the potato shape from a tagboard template. (See figure 7.6.) Illustrate the book and write a story or dictate it to the teacher. Use the key words for an independent writing experience.

Leprechaun Wishes

Write wishes on slips of paper. "I will be a good friend" and "I will read a book" are some examples of wishes. Place the wishes in a black plastic kettle for the leprechaun to find. Children may take turns being the leprechaun and seeing if they can perform that wish.

Fig. 7.6. Potato shape book directions and pattern.

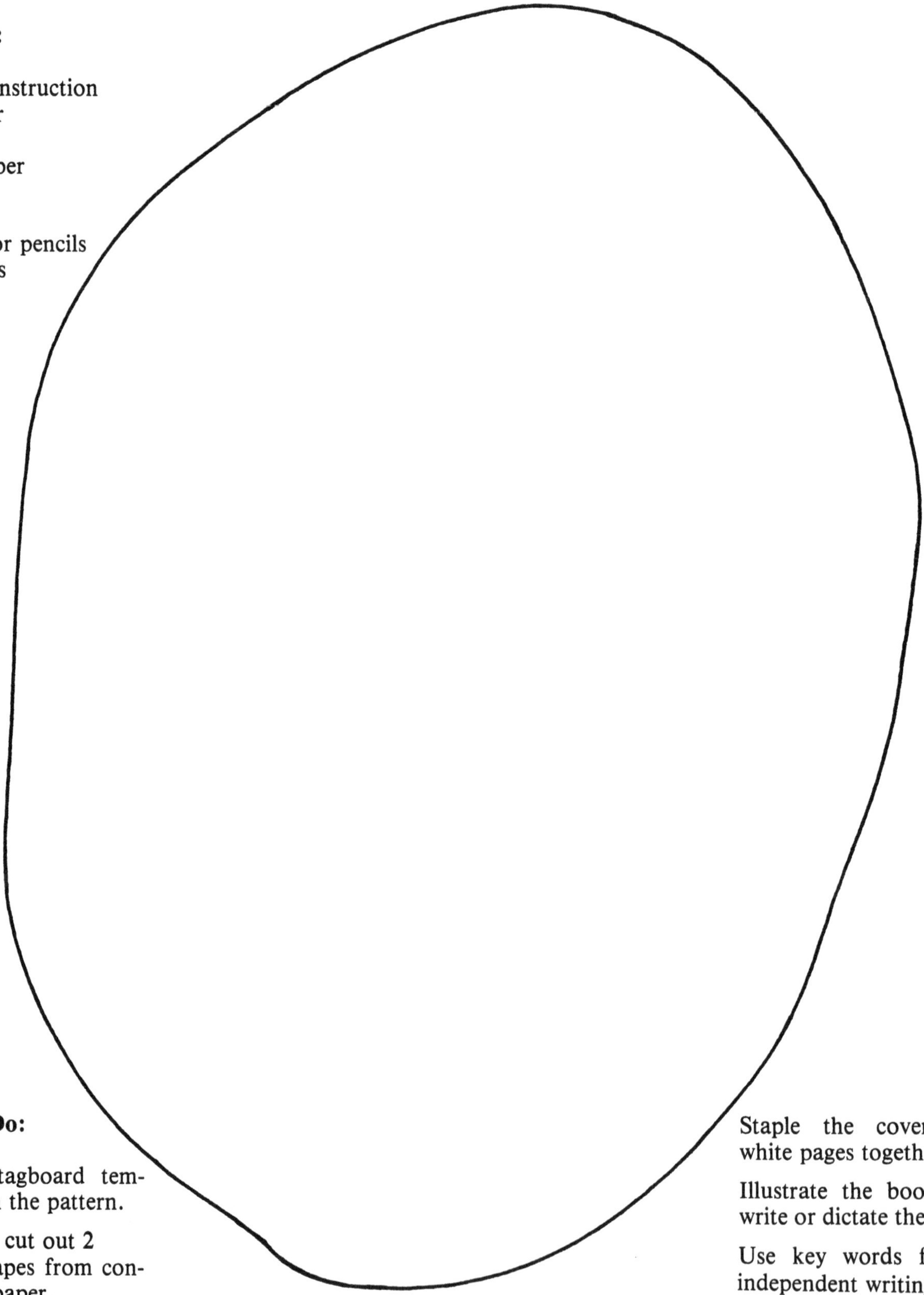

Materials:

Brown construction
      paper
Tagboard
White paper
Scissors
Stapler
Markers or pencils
Key words

What to Do:

Make a tagboard template from the pattern.

Trace and cut out 2 potato shapes from construction paper.

Teacher may precut white pages.

Staple the cover and white pages together.

Illustrate the book and write or dictate the story.

Use key words for an independent writing experience.

COOPERATIVE/GROUP EXPERIENCE

Butterflies

Read *The Irish Piper* by Jim Latimer. (See bibliography on page 118.) In this retelling of the tale of the Pied Piper, the piper's music sounded like butterflies to the children. Cut paper into butterfly shapes. Create butterflies by making ink-blot designs on the pieces of paper. (See figure 7.7.) Display the butterflies on a wall.

Blarney Stones

Read *Fin M'Coul: The Giant of Knockmany Hill* by Tomie dePaola. Fin was so strong he could squeeze water out of a stone.

Make blarney stones for a St. Patrick's Day celebration. In a saucepan, heat 2 cups salt and 2 cups water until salt is dissolved. Mix 2 cups of cold water and 2 cups of cornstarch together and add to the salt and water mixture. Cook the mixture over low heat until it forms a ball. Remove the mixture from the heat, let it cool, and then knead. Make individual blarney stones. The stones will harden in one to two days.

Magic Dust

Read *Clever Tom and the Leprechaun* by Linda Shute. In this retelling of an Irish folktale, Clever Tom captures a leprechaun, who leads him on a trail to find the pot of gold.

Make a trail of magic dust to follow on St. Patrick's Day. Use green glitter as magic dust and spread a trail throughout the classroom. Have a special treat or surprise at the end of the trail.

Fig. 7.7. Butterfly shape pattern.

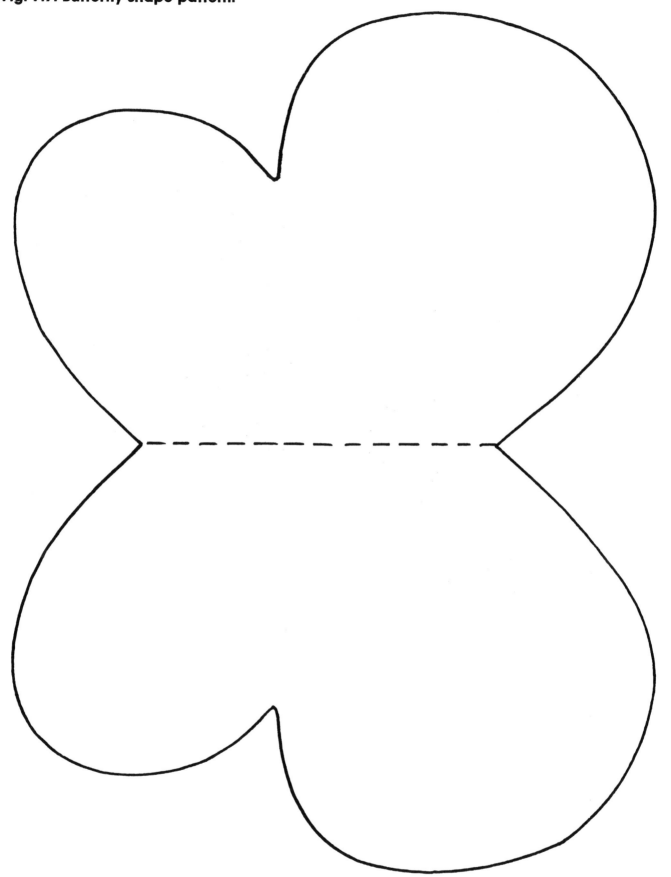

ART/CRAFT EXPERIENCE

Tempera Painting

Leprechauns are central to many stories about Ireland and St. Patrick's Day. Read *Tim O'Toole and the Wee Folk* by Gerald McDermott. In this Irish tale, a band of leprechauns helps Tim and his wife make their fortune. In Lorna Balian's *Leprechauns Never Lie*, a lazy girl catches a leprechaun. The illustrations are in shades of brown with a green leprechaun on each page. (See bibliography on page 118.) Create a leprechaun using green tempera paint. Write a caption for the leprechaun painting. Display the paintings on the walls or the bulletin board. Bind the paintings together to make a class book.

Color Mixing

The color green is closely associated with St. Patrick's Day. Create the color green in a variety of ways. Add yellow and blue food coloring to water to make green. Use blue and yellow finger paint to create green. Use glue diluted in water and a brush to make a collage with yellow and blue tissue paper. Look through yellow and blue cellophane.

Leprechaun Play Dough

Make leprechaun play dough by mixing 1¼ cups flour, ¼ cup salt, 1½ tablespoons oil, 1 package lime gelatin, and 1 cup boiling water. Knead the play dough when it cools. Use shamrock cookie cutters and other St. Patrick's Day shapes with the play dough.

COOKING/MATH EXPERIENCE

St. Patrick's Day Tasting Party

Have a St. Patrick's Day tasting party to sample a variety of green foods. Taste celery, pickles, spinach, peas, olives, and other green foods. Make a graph to determine favorite green foods.

Shamrock Sandwiches

Enjoy a St. Patrick's Day treat by spreading cream cheese tinted with green food coloring on white bread. Use a cookie cutter to cut the sandwiches into shamrock shapes. (See figure 7.8.)

Irish Wonders

Make Irish Wonders by sifting 4 cups powdered sugar onto waxed paper. Mix ⅔ cup sweetened condensed milk, 3 drops green food coloring, and ¼ teaspoon peppermint flavoring together. Add the powdered sugar to the mixture gradually. Knead with your hands until smooth. Form the mixture into small balls and place them on the waxed paper. Refrigerate for a few hours and eat.

Fig. 7.8. Shamrock-shaped sandwich.

2 slices bread

spread
green
cream
cheese

make a sandwich

cut shamrock
shape

Favorite Potato Foods

Read *Jamie O'Rourke and the Big Potato* by Tomie dePaola. (See bibliography on page 118.) Taste a variety of potato products, such as potato sticks, potato chips, mashed potatoes, and raw potatoes. Have each child select a favorite potato product and make a graph to determine the class's overall favorite.

Leprechaun Gumdrops

Make leprechaun gumdrops by pouring a box of lime gelatin into a small bowl. Slowly squeeze six drops of water onto the same spot with an eyedropper. Make sure each drop soaks in before adding the next drop. Place a fork under the wet area and lift up. The gumdrop that has formed will come up to the top.

SCIENCE/DISCOVERY EXPERIENCE

Discovery Museum

Create a discovery museum to display contributions, collections, and books about St. Patrick's Day and Ireland. Display the items on a table, shelf, or counter top in the classroom. Use a sentence strip to label the items. Explore the museum with a group or individually.

Lucky Clover

Finding a four-leaved clover is thought to bring good luck to the finder. Purchase a four-leaved clover plant from a nursery or grow clover by planting clover seeds in clear plastic cups filled with potting soil. Watch the clover grow and be sure to look for those special four-leaved clovers.

Shamrock Hunt

Go on a shamrock hunt. Find a clover-covered patch in a yard or field. Make a telescope to take along on your hunt. Use an empty paper tube and cover one end with green cellophane. Secure the cellophane with a rubber band. Poke holes at the other end and attach a string so that the telescope can be worn around the neck.

Sprouting Potatoes

In *Jamie O'Rourke and the Big Potato* by Tomie dePaola, a leprechaun leaves Jamie with a potato seed instead of the traditional pot of gold. (See bibliography on page 118.) Sprout a potato by putting it in a bag and placing it in a dark cabinet or closet. The potato should begin to sprout within a few days. Place the sprouting potato in a shoe box. Cut a small circle at one end of the lid. Place the cover on the box and set it in a sunny window. As the sprouts grow, they will seek the sunlight and grow through the hole in the box.

From *Holiday Story Play*, copyright 1993. Libraries Unlimited/Teacher Ideas Press, P.O. Box 6633, Englewood, CO 80155-6633.

MUSIC/GAME EXPERIENCE

Follow the Piper

Play "Follow the Piper" music performed by Pamela Copus. (See bibliography on this page.) Select one child to be the piper. The remaining children follow the piper and mimic his or her movements.

Greenie Meanie

Have the children form a circle and place a paper "greenie meanie" bag in the center. Select a child to find a green object to put inside. That child then chooses someone else to find something green to go inside the greenie meanie bag. The game continues until all the children have contributed something to the bag.

BIBLIOGRAPHY

Balian, Lorna. *Leprechauns Never Lie.* Nashville, TN: Abingdon Press, 1980.

Barth, Edna. *Shamrocks, Harps, and Shillelaghs.* New York: Clarion Books, 1977.

Bunting, Eve. *St. Patrick's Day in the Morning.* New York: Clarion Books, 1980.

dePaola, Tomie. *Fin M'Coul: The Giant of Knockmany Hill.* New York: Holiday House, 1981.

_____. *Jamie O'Rourke and the Big Potato.* New York: G. P. Putnam's Sons, 1992.

Kessel, Joyce K. *St. Patrick's Day.* Minneapolis, MN: Carolrhoda Books, 1982.

Latimer, Jim. *The Irish Piper.* New York: Charles Scribner's Sons, 1991.

McDermott, Gerald. *Daniel O'Rourke.* New York: Puffin Books, 1986.

_____. *Tim O'Toole and the Wee Folk.* New York: Puffin Books, 1990.

Shute, Linda. *Clever Tom and the Leprechaun.* New York: Scholastic, 1988.

Music

Copus, Pamela, and Joyce Harlow. "Follow the Piper." *Holiday Story Play Music.* Plano, TX: Dreamtime Productions, P.O. Box 940061, Plano, TX 75094-0061.

EASTER

DRAMA/PLAY EXPERIENCE

Read *The Runaway Bunny* by Margaret Wise Brown to introduce the theme of Easter. (See bibliography on page 137.) Little Bunny decides he no longer wants to be a bunny and tries to run away, but Mother Bunny manages to find him. Demonstrate the simpletees costumes and play props.

Simpletees Costumes

Use the simpletees costumes of the runaway bunny and the mother bunny for a dramatic play experience. (See figures 8.1 and 8.2.)

Play Props

Play props can include a fishing pole, rubber boots, gardening gloves, a straw hat, a plastic tree branch, a rocking chair, and plastic carrots.

Face Masks

Create face masks of the runaway bunny and the mother bunny. Use tagboard templates and trace the different characters. (See figures 8.3 and 8.4.)

Stick Puppets/Paper Bag Theater

Make stick puppets of the runaway bunny and the mother bunny. (See figure 8.5.) Create a paper bag theater for the stick puppets. (See figure 1.5 on page 6.) Present the story of the runaway bunny and his mother to a friend or take home to present to families.

(Text continues on page 125.)

Fig. 8.1. Simpletees costumes: Easter.

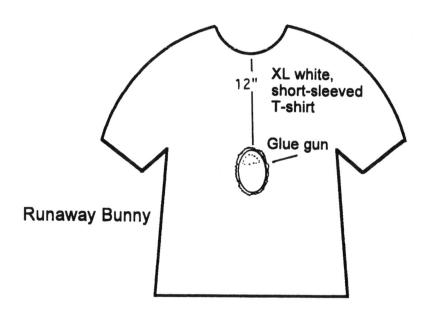

Runaway Bunny

Mother Bunny

Glue gun 1 1/4 yd. lace ruffle
to bottom of T-shirt

Fig. 8.2. Bunny tail pattern and directions.

Materials:

⅛ yard white fake fur
Scissors
Glue gun

What to Do:

Use the pattern and cut out 2 fur tails (cut on back side).

Glue gun tails to center back of T-shirts 12" down from the neck.

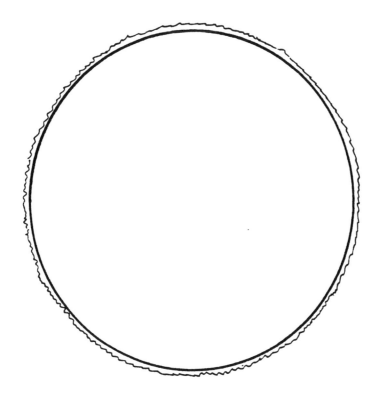

Fig. 8.3. Runaway Bunny face mask pattern.

Fig. 8.4. Mother Bunny face mask pattern.

Fig. 8.5. Easter stick puppet patterns.

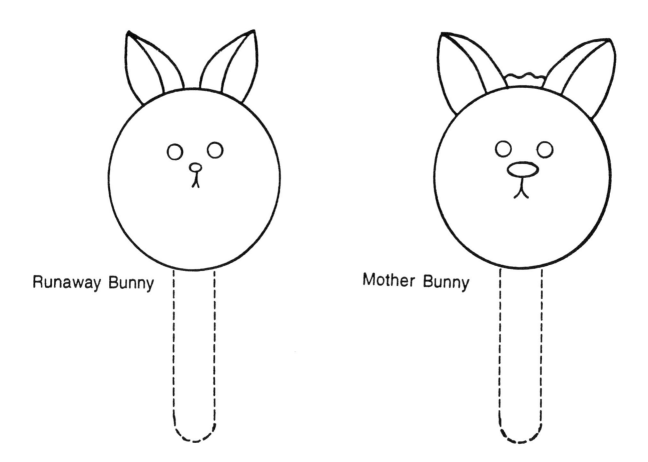

Runaway Bunny

Mother Bunny

LITERATURE/WRITING EXPERIENCE

Easter *Versions*

Share a variety of books about Easter. For example, *Easter* by Gail Gibbons and Edna Barth's *Lilies, Rabbits, and Painted Eggs* tell how the customs surrounding Easter came about. *An Easter Alphabet* by Nora Tarlow is illustrated by a variety of artists from the past. (See bibliography on pages 137-38.)

Easter *Children's Version*

Write a children's version about Easter on a large sheet of chart paper.

Key-Word Books and Key Words

Make a key-word book with the unique or important words from *The Runaway Bunny* by Margaret Wise Brown. (See bibliography on page 137.) The key words for *The Runaway Bunny* are as follows:

bunny	runaway	mother
little	fish	rock
crocus	bird	sailboat
circus	boy	carrot

Crocus Shape Book

Make a crocus shape book by tracing the crocus shape from a tagboard template. (See figure 8.6.) Illustrate the book and write a story or dictate it to the teacher. Use the key words for an independent writing experience.

Easter Cards

Read *Euclid Bunny Delivers the Mail* by Bruce Koscielniak. Euclid is just too quick when it comes to delivering the mail, and must correct his mistakes in a hurry. (See bibliography on page 138.) Write and decorate Easter cards or notes to friends or family members.

Imaginary Friend

John Burningham's *Aldo* is the tale of a little girl's imaginary friend, who just happens to be a rabbit. (See bibliography on page 137.) Illustrate a picture of what your imaginary friend would look like. Write or dictate a caption about the imaginary friend.

Fig. 8.6. Crocus shape book directions and pattern.

Materials:

Blue construction paper   Stapler
Tagboard   Markers or pencils
White paper   Key words
Scissors

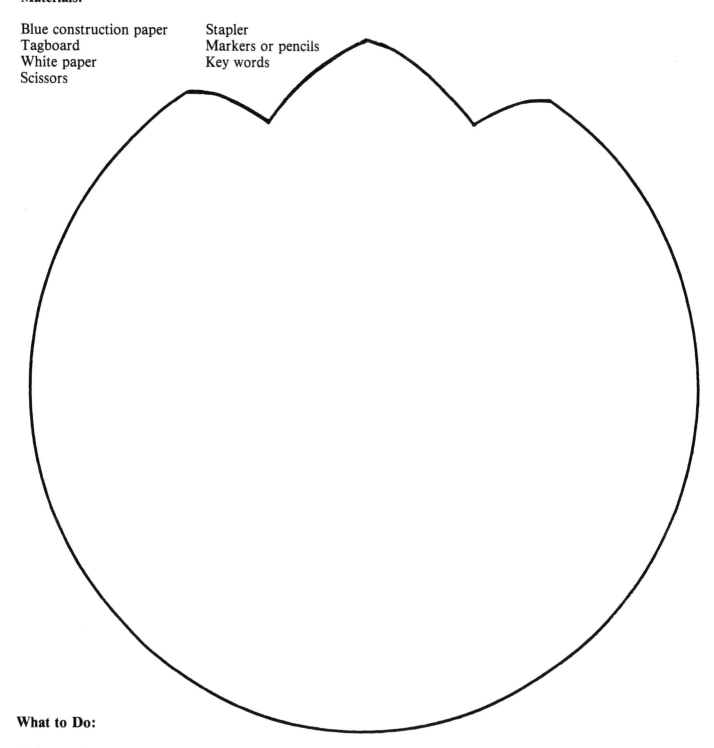

What to Do:

Make a tagboard template from the pattern.

Trace and cut out 2 crocus shapes from construction paper.

Teacher may precut white pages.

Staple the cover and white pages together.

Illustrate the book and write or dictate the story.

Use key words for an independent writing experience.

COOPERATIVE/GROUP EXPERIENCE

Bunny Parade

Read *Easter Parade* by Mary Chalmers. The Easter animals fill their baskets with decorated eggs, flowers, and candy and then begin their Easter parade. (See bibliography on page 137.) Plan a bunny parade. Make bunny feet out of construction paper. (See figure 8.7.) March to "Bunny Parade" by Pamela Copus and Joyce Harlow in *Holiday Story Play Music*. (See bibliography on page 138.)

Above and Below Mural

Humbug Rabbit by Lorna Balian is an Easter story told in two parts—one story takes place above ground while the other takes place below ground. (See bibliography on page 137.) Create a mural depicting the events that take place above and below ground.

Red Wings

Read *The Little Rabbit Who Wanted Red Wings* by Carolyn Sherwin Bailey. (See bibliography on page 137.) Rabbits do not usually have red wings, but this little rabbit's wish comes true. Make red wings. (See figure 8.8.) Fill a plastic swimming pool with water and look at the reflection in the water while wearing the wings.

Fig. 8.7. Bunny feet pattern and directions.

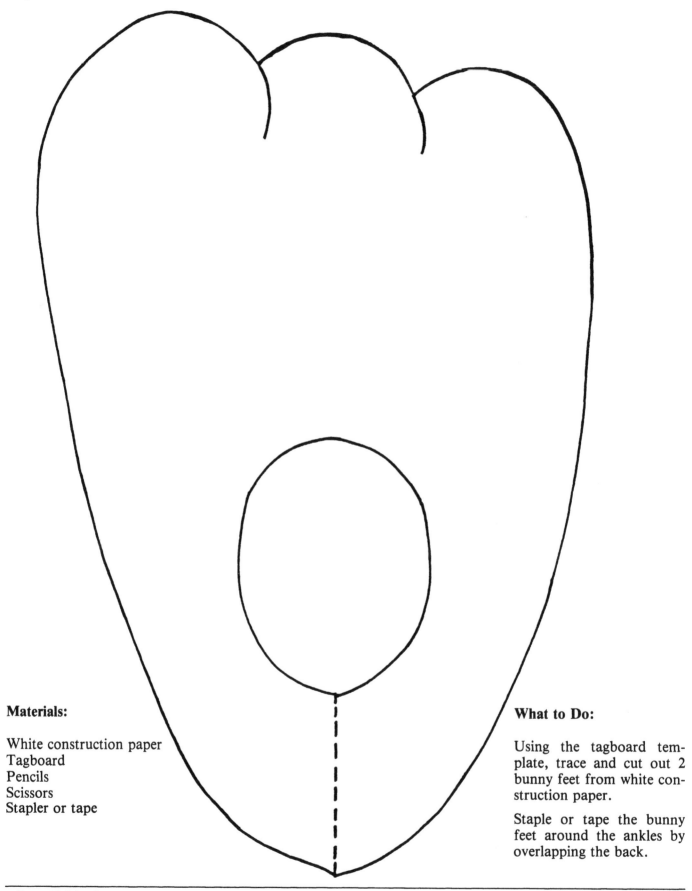

Materials:

White construction paper
Tagboard
Pencils
Scissors
Stapler or tape

What to Do:

Using the tagboard template, trace and cut out 2 bunny feet from white construction paper.

Staple or tape the bunny feet around the ankles by overlapping the back.

Fig. 8.8. Red wings directions and pattern.

Materials:

Tagboard
Red construction paper
Scissors
Markers or pencils
Stapler or tape

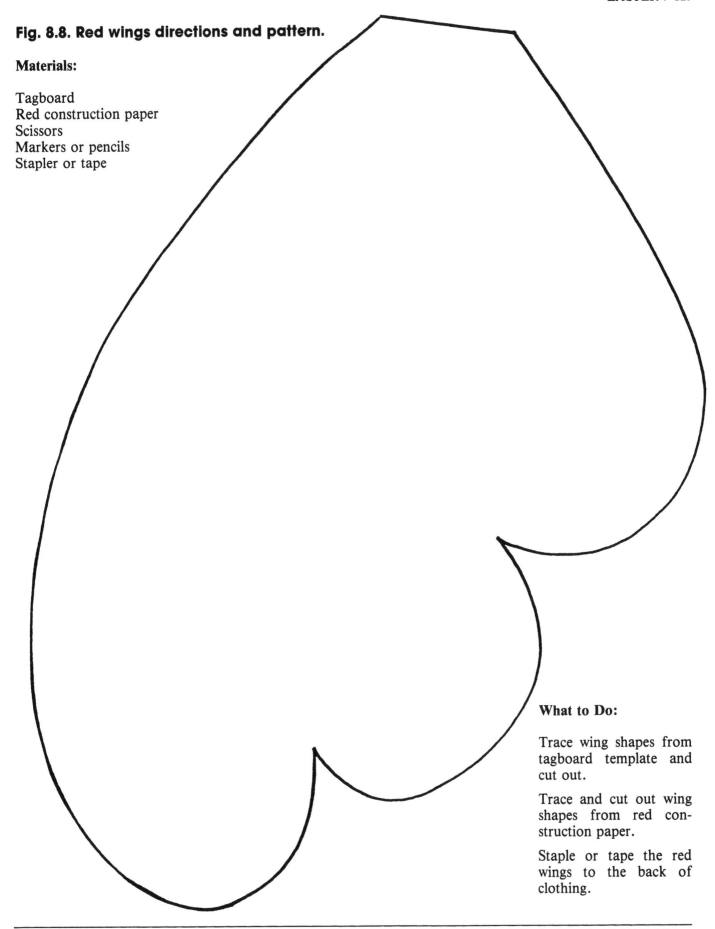

What to Do:

Trace wing shapes from tagboard template and cut out.

Trace and cut out wing shapes from red construction paper.

Staple or tape the red wings to the back of clothing.

ART/CRAFT EXPERIENCE

Tempera Painting

Read *The Runaway Bunny* by Margaret Wise Brown. (See bibliography on page 137.) Use white, blue, green, and orange tempera paint to paint a picture of the runaway bunny and his mother. Write a caption for the painting. Display the paintings on the walls or the bulletin board. Bind the paintings together to make a class book.

Easter Bunny

The Easter bunny is found wherever Easter is celebrated. Read *The Easter Bunny* by Agnes Mathieu, in which many reasons for believing in the Easter bunny are shared. (See bibliography on page 138.) What do you think the Easter bunny looks like? Paint a picture to illustrate.

Decorating Easter Eggs

Decorating eggs for Easter is a traditional part of the Easter celebration. In *The Easter Egg Artists* by Adrienne Adams, Orson Abbott has fun decorating eggs and much more. (See bibliography on page 137.) Decorate hard boiled eggs by pouring hot water into a cup. Add a tablespoon of white vinegar and food coloring. Dip the eggs into the food coloring mixture and place them in an empty egg carton to dry. Have an Easter egg hunt.

Dinosaur Easter Eggs

Read *The Great Big Especially Beautiful Easter Egg* by James Stevenson and Bernard Most's *Happy Holidaysaurus!* (See bibliography on page 138.) Imagine what it would be like to decorate a dinosaur egg for Easter. Draw a picture to illustrate what your egg would look like.

Easter Bonnets

People have long celebrated Easter and the beginning of spring by wearing new clothes. Read *Chicken Sunday* by Patricia Polacco. In this story from the author's childhood, three friends were able to buy Gramma Eula that special Easter bonnet by decorating Easter eggs. (See bibliography on page 138.) Make paper-plate Easter hats to celebrate the arrival of spring. (See figure 8.9.)

Fig. 8.9. Easter hat directions.

Materials:

Paper plates (plain)
Scissors
Art tissue
Ribbon or paper streamers
Glue

What to Do:

Cut out the center section of the paper plate.

Cut 3" squares of assorted color art tissue and round off the corners to make a flower shape.

Glue the tissue flowers around the brim of the hat.

Add ribbon or streamers with glue, tape, or staples.

COOKING/MATH EXPERIENCE

Bunny Brunch Foods

Bunnies like to eat a variety of foods. Taste foods such as carrots, lettuce, turnips, green peppers, and sprouts. Make a graph to determine the favorite bunny foods.

Easter Egg Basket

Make Easter egg baskets with cookies, icing, coconut, and jelly beans by following the recipe in figure 8.10.

Hot Cross Buns

See Edna Barth's *Lilies, Rabbits, and Painted Eggs* for the story behind spicy buns with raisins. Make hot cross buns by following the recipe in figure 8.11.

A Coney Tale

Rabbits were known as *coneys* in seventeenth-century Flanders. Read *A Coney Tale* by Paul Ratz de Tagyos to discover what happens when the coneys dig up the biggest carrots in the world. (See bibliography on page 138.) Conclude *A Coney Tale* by tasting a variety of carrot products, such as raw carrots, carrot juice, and cooked carrots.

Fig. 8.10. Easter egg basket.

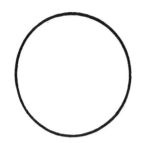

1 sugar cookie

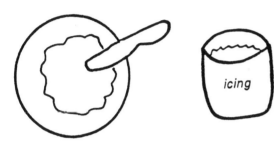

spread icing

sprinkle coconut

add 5 jelly bean eggs

Fig. 8.11. Hot cross buns.

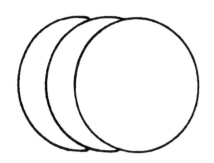

separate
flaky biscuits

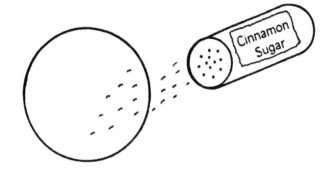

sprinkle on
cinnamon sugar

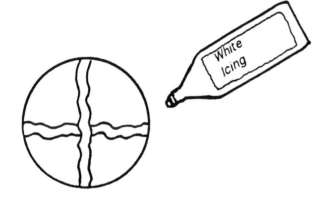

squeeze a cross
shape on biscuit
with white icing

bake at 425° for 10
minutes

SCIENCE/DISCOVERY EXPERIENCE

Discovery Museum

Create a discovery museum to display collections, contributions, and books about Easter. Display the items on a table, shelf, or counter top in the classroom. Use sentence strips to label the items. Explore the museum in a group or individually.

Rabbits

Rabbits are an important part of the Easter tradition. Learn how real rabbits grow by reading *See How They Grow: Rabbit* by Barrie Watts. (See bibliography on page 138.)

Hatching Eggs

Eggs are decorated and hidden as part of Easter celebrations around the world. Crack an egg open and empty the contents onto a saucer. Examine the different part of the egg. Several books offer photographs and drawings to help children investigate the life cycle of the egg. *Inside an Egg* by Sylvia A. Johnson uses photographs to take the reader through the stages of the egg. *Chickens Aren't the Only Ones* by Ruth Heller describes a variety of animals that are hatched from eggs. *See How They Grow: Chick* by Jane Burton also takes the reader from egg to chick. (See bibliography on page 137.)

What's Inside Your Egg?

Several books detail what happens to eggs at Easter time. In *Rechenka's Eggs* by Patricia Polacco, Babushka is surprised by one of her beautifully decorated eggs. The rabbits receive a surprise after they decorate some old eggs in *Happy Easter* by Kurt Wiese. The lonely little bunny in *The Golden Egg Book* by Margaret Wise Brown wonders what is inside the egg he found. (See bibliography on pages 137-38.) Pretend you found an egg outside. What is inside your egg? Draw a picture to illustrate.

Bunny Tails

Read *Pat the Bunny* by Dorothy Kunhardt. (See bibliography on page 138.) Make a texture book about a bunny. Use a cotton ball for a soft tail, corduroy for a rough tail, and satin for a smooth tail. (See figure 8.12.)

Fig. 8.12. Bunny tails directions and pattern.

Materials:

Tagboard
9" X 12" white construction
 paper
Stapler
Cotton balls, satin, and
 corduroy
Glue

What to Do:

Trace and cut out rabbit
shapes from tagboard
template.

Cut out 3 bunny shapes and
staple together to make a
book.

Cut out and glue circle
shapes of different textures
for tails.

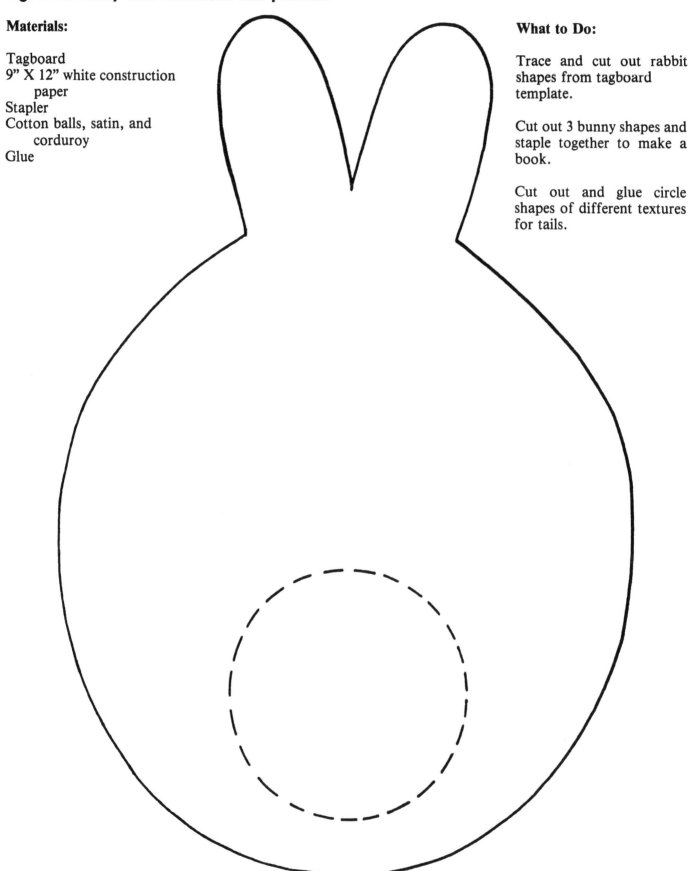

MUSIC/GAME EXPERIENCE

To Rabbit Town

Read *To Rabbittown* by April Halprin Wayland. (See bibliography on page 138.) Pretend to become a rabbit as the little girl does in the story.

Bunny Hop

Read *The Bunny Hop* by Teddy Slater. (See bibliography on page 138.) Buddy Rabbit learns to count and do the bunny hop at the same time. Do the bunny hop around the classroom.

Egg Relay

Celebrate Easter by having an egg relay. Roll hardboiled eggs across the floor, using straws or plastic spoons.

The Bunny Trail

Hop down the bunny trail. Create an obstacle course on the playground. Practice hopping around the trail.

BIBLIOGRAPHY

Adams, Adrienne. *The Easter Egg Artists.* New York: Aladdin Books, 1976.

Bailey, Carolyn Sherwin. *The Little Rabbit Who Wanted Red Wings.* New York: Platt & Munk, 1978.

Balian, Lorna. *Humbug Rabbit.* Nashville, TN: Abingdon Press, 1974.

Barth, Edna. *Lilies, Rabbits, and Painted Eggs.* New York: Seabury Press, 1970.

Brown, Margaret Wise. *The Golden Egg Book.* Racine, WI: Western, 1947.

_____. *The Runaway Bunny.* New York: Harper Trophy, 1942.

Burningham, John. *Aldo.* New York: Crown, 1991.

Burton, Jane. *See How They Grow: Chick.* New York: Lodestar Books, 1992.

Chalmers, Mary. *Easter Parade.* New York: Harper Trophy, 1988.

Gibbons, Gail. *Easter.* New York: Holiday House, 1989.

Heller, Ruth. *Chickens Aren't the Only Ones.* New York: Scholastic, 1981.

Johnson, Sylvia A. *Inside an Egg.* Minneapolis, MN: Lerner Publications, 1982.

From *Holiday Story Play*, copyright 1993. Libraries Unlimited/Teacher Ideas Press, P.O. Box 6633, Englewood, CO 80155-6633.

Koscielniak, Bruce. *Euclid Bunny Delivers the Mail.* New York: Alfred A. Knopf, 1991.

Kunhardt, Dorothy. *Pat the Bunny.* New York: Western, 1942.

Mathieu, Agnes. *The Easter Bunny.* New York: Dial Books for Young Readers, 1986.

Most, Bernard. *Happy Holidaysaurus!* San Diego, CA: Harcourt Brace Jovanovich, 1992.

Polacco, Patricia. *Chicken Sunday.* New York: Philomel Books, 1992.

———. *Rechenka's Eggs.* New York: Philomel Books, 1988.

Ratz de Tagyos, Paul. *A Coney Tale.* New York: Clarion Books, 1992.

Slater, Teddy. *The Bunny Hop.* New York: Scholastic, 1992.

Stevenson, James. *The Great Big Especially Beautiful Easter Egg.* New York: Mulberry Books, 1983.

Tarlow, Nora. *An Easter Alphabet.* New York: G. P. Putnam's Sons, 1991.

Watts, Barrie. *See How They Grow: Rabbit.* New York: Lodestar Books, 1992.

Wayland, April Halprin. *To Rabbittown.* New York: Scholastic, 1989.

Wiese, Kurt. *Happy Easter.* New York: Puffin Books, 1952.

Music

Copus, Pamela, and Joyce Harlow. "Bunny Parade." *Holiday Story Play Music.* Plano, TX: Dreamtime Productions, P.O. Box 940061, Plano, TX 75094-0061.

MOTHER'S DAY

DRAMA/PLAY EXPERIENCE

Read *A Mother for Choco* by Keiko Kasza to introduce the theme of Mother's Day. (See bibliography on page 151.) Choco is a little bird who is all alone in the world. He wants a mother and searches for someone who looks just like him. Choco finally finds his mother—someone to hug and kiss and play with him. Demonstrate the simpletees costumes and play props.

Simpletees Costumes

Use the simpletees costumes of Choco and Mother Bear for a dramatic play experience. (See figures 9.1, 9.2, and 9.3.)

Play Props

Play props can include an apron, plastic apples, a small rocking chair, a small table, chairs, and dishes.

Face Masks

Create face masks of Choco and Mother Bear. Use tagboard templates and trace the different characters. (See figures 9.4 and 9.5.)

Stick Puppets/Paper Bag Theater

Make stick puppets of Choco and Mother Bear. (See figure 9.6.) Create a paper bag theater for the stick puppets. (See figure 1.5 on page 6.) Present the story of Choco and Mother Bear to a friend or families.

(Text continues on page 146.)

Fig. 9.1. Simpletees costumes: Mother's Day.

Choco

Glue gun

XL yellow,
short-sleeved
T-shirt

Mother Bear

XL brown,
short-sleeved
T-shirt

12"

Glue gun

Fig. 9.2. Choco's wing directions and pattern.

Materials:

¼ yard dark blue
craft felt
Scissors
Glue gun

What to Do:

Place wing pattern on the fold and cut out.

Glue gun the wings to the back of the neck of a yellow, XL short-sleeved T-shirt (approximately 2" down from the neck band.)

Fig. 9.3. Mother Bear tail directions and pattern.

Materials:

⅛ yard brown fake fur
Scissors
Glue gun

What to Do:

Use tail pattern to cut out the fur tail (cut from the back side.)

Glue gun the tail to the center back of an XL, brown, short-sleeved T-shirt (approximately 12" down from neck).

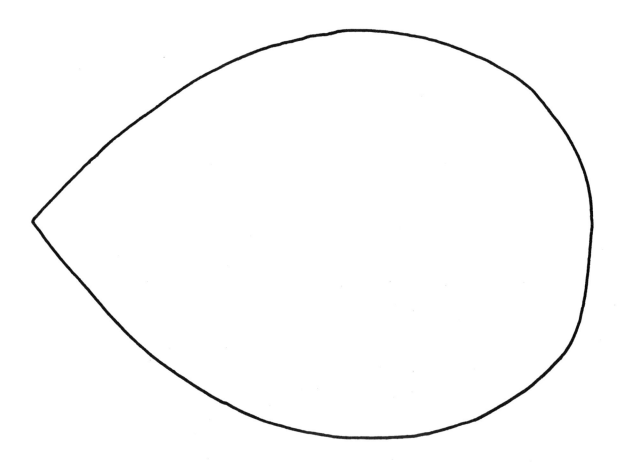

Fig. 9.4. Choco face mask pattern.

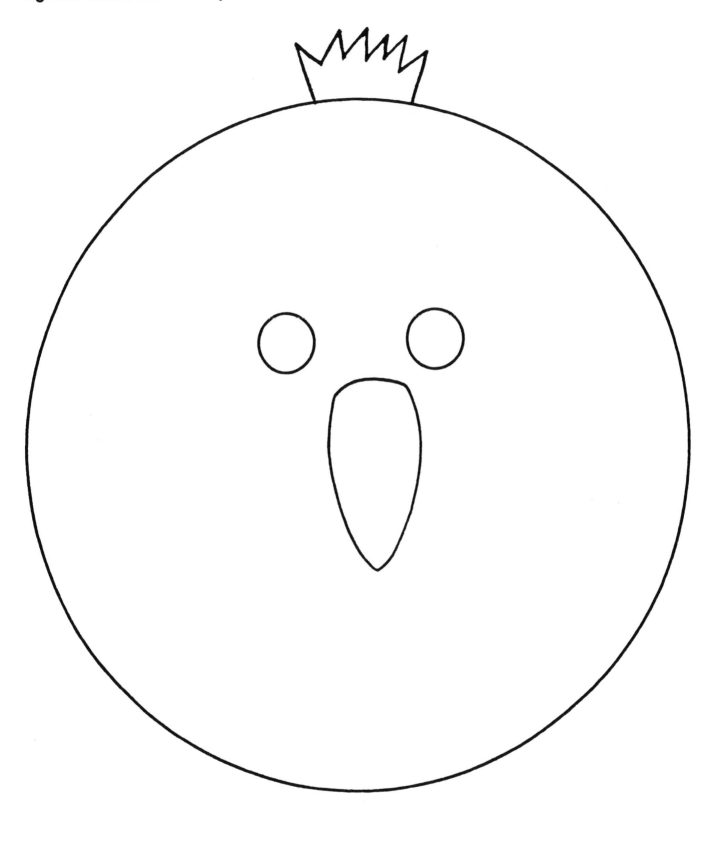

Fig. 9.5. Mother Bear face mask pattern.

Fig. 9.6. Mother's Day stick puppet patterns.

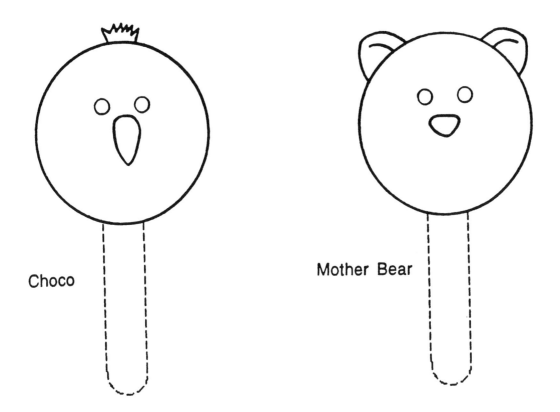

Choco

Mother Bear

LITERATURE/WRITING EXPERIENCE

Mother's Day *Versions*

Experience a variety of stories about Mother's Day. For example, *Happy Mother's Day* by Steven Kroll is the delightful story of the special Mother's Day gifts Dad and the children give to Mom. In Harriet Ziefert's *What Is Mother's Day?*, Little Mouse and his father create a special Mother's Day. Hazel the mouse goes to visit her mother in *Mother's Mother's Day* by Lorna Balian. *The Mother's Day Mice* by Eve Bunting also shows mice celebrate Mother's Day in a special way. (See bibliography on page 151.)

Mother's Day *Children's Version*

Write a children's version about Mother's Day on a large sheet of chart paper.

Key-Word Books and Key Words

Make a key-word book with the unique or important words from *A Mother for Choco* by Keiko Kasza. (See bibliography on page 151.) The key words for *A Mother for Choco* are as follows:

Mother	Choco	giraffe
penguin	walrus	bear
kiss	sing	dance
apple		

Hat Shape Book

Make a hat shape book by tracing the hat shape from a tagboard template. (See figure 9.7.) Illustrate the book and write a story or dictate it to the teacher. Use the key words for an independent writing experience.

A Mother for Me

Read *A Mother for Choco* by Keiko Kasza. (See bibliography on page 151.) Draw a picture to answer the question, "If you had a mommy, what would she do?" Write or dictate a response on the illustration. Combine the illustrations for a class book. Title the book *A Mother for Me*.

Happy Mother's Day

Steven Kroll's *Happy Mother's Day* describes the different gifts that the children give to their moms. (See bibliography on page 151.) Tell what you will give or do for your mother or guardian on Mother's Day. Write the responses on a large sheet of chart paper.

Fig. 9.7. Mother's hat shape book directions and pattern.

Materials:

Yellow construction paper
Tagboard
White paper
Scissors
Stapler
Markers or pencils
Key words

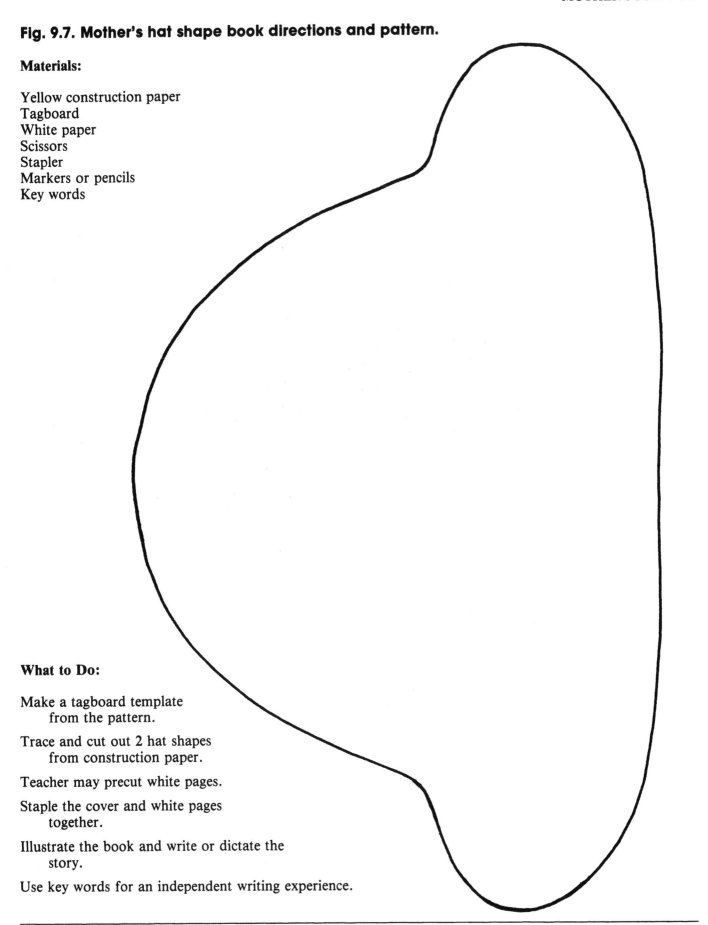

What to Do:

Make a tagboard template
from the pattern.

Trace and cut out 2 hat shapes
from construction paper.

Teacher may precut white pages.

Staple the cover and white pages
together.

Illustrate the book and write or dictate the
story.

Use key words for an independent writing experience.

This Is My Mother

Read *This Quiet Lady* by Charlotte Zolotow. In this story, a little girl talks about different photographs of her mother. (See bibliography on page 151.) Bring a photograph of your mother or caregiver to school. Write or dictate a description of the picture.

COOPERATIVE/GROUP EXPERIENCE

The Maybe Garden

Read *The Maybe Garden* by Kimberly Burke-Weiner, in which a little boy describes his mother's garden. (See bibliography on page 151.) When the mother suggests that he plant his own garden, he describes a "maybe garden" that he might plant. Discuss what you would plant in your "maybe garden." Work in small groups and paint a mural of the "maybe garden," using cake tempera paints and water.

Tell Me a Story

Read *Tell Me a Story, Mama* by Angela Johnson. (See bibliography on page 151). While getting ready for bed, mother and daughter share stories from the mother's childhood memories. Share a memory from your mother's or female relative's childhood with the class.

ART/CRAFT EXPERIENCE

Tempera Painting

In *A Mother for Choco* by Keiko Kasza, a little bird searches and finds the perfect mother. (See bibliography on page 151.) Use yellow, blue, brown, and green tempera paint to paint a picture of Choco and Mother Bear. Write a caption for the painting. Display the paintings on the walls or the bulletin board. Bind the paintings together to make a class book.

Stargazing Sky

Read *Stargazing Sky* by Deborah Kogan Ray and capture the special relationship between mother and daughter. (See bibliography on page 151.) Make a stargazing sky for your mother or special adult. Use dark blue construction paper and gummed stars to create a Milky Way, the North Star, the Big Dipper, and a shooting star.

COOKING/MATH EXPERIENCE

Mother's Day Tea

In *What Is Mother's Day?* by Harriet Ziefert, Little Mouse and his father make Mother's Day very special. (See bibliography on page 151.) Plan a very special Mother's Day Tea and send a special invitation to your mother or guardian. Prepare hot tea and Mother's Day cookies by following the recipe in figure 9.8.

Fig. 9.8. Mother's Day cookies recipe.

1 package lemon cake mix

½ cup vegetable oil

2 tablespoons water

2 eggs

Mix ingredients and drop by teaspoonful on a cookie sheet. Sprinkle on confectioner's sugar and bake 350° for 10 to 12 minutes.

Mother's Day Surprises

Create a unique treat for Mother's Day by making Mother's Day Surprises. Mix ½ cup honey, ½ cup peanut butter, ½ cup cocoa, and 1 cup wheat germ in a bowl. Roll the mixture into little balls and hide a peanut inside. Then roll the balls in coconut and refrigerate.

SCIENCE/DISCOVERY EXPERIENCE

Discovery Museum

Create a discovery museum to display photographs of mothers. Have the children bring a photograph of their mothers or adult female relatives from home. Display the photographs on a bulletin board in the classroom. Explore the photographs with a group or individually.

Mother's Day Bath Salts

In *The Mother's Day Mice* by Eve Bunting, three little mice search for a special present for their mother. (See bibliography on page 151.) Make a special present of bath salts. Mix 1 tablespoon glycerin, two drops food coloring, and perfume together. Place 3 cups Epsom salts in a large container and add the glycerin mixture. Stir the bath salts until completely mixed and place ¼ cup into a sealed plastic bag. (The bath salts should make enough for 12 gifts.) Place the bag of bath salts inside a special Mother's Day card.

Sachet Bags

Read *Mother's Mother's Day* by Lorna Balian. Hazel the mouse plans to visit her mother on Mother's Day, but Hazel's mother has gone to visit her own mother. (See bibliography on page 151.) Make sachet bags for your mother, grandmother, or special female relative or guardian. Collect flowers and let them dry out, or use potpourri. Make sachet bags out of netting or fabric. Cut a 6-inch square of netting. Place potpourri in the center of the square. Turn up the edges and secure them with a ribbon tied in a bow.

MUSIC/GAME EXPERIENCE

Music of the Morning

Read *Mara in the Morning* by C. B. Christiansen. Mara loves the silent, soothing music of the morning and discovers that her mother does too. Listen to "Music of the Morning" by Pamela Copus and Joyce Harlow in *Holiday Story Play Music*. (See bibliography on page 151.) While listening to the music, see how quietly you can walk, so that you would not wake anyone up. Listen to the sounds around you.

I Love You

In *Mama, Do You Love Me?* by Barbara M. Joosse, a mother tells her little daughter that she loves her more than a raven loves his treasure, a dog loves his tail, and a whale loves his spout. See how many similar comparisons the class can make, such as "I love you more than a cat loves her milk."

BIBLIOGRAPHY

Balian, Lorna. *Mother's Mother's Day.* Nashville, TN: Abingdon Press, 1982.

Bunting, Eve. *The Mother's Day Mice.* New York: Clarion Books, 1986.

Burke-Weiner, Kimberly. *The Maybe Garden.* Hillsboro, OR: Beyond Words, 1992.

Christiansen, C. B. *Mara in the Morning.* New York: Atheneum, 1991.

Johnson, Angela. *Tell Me a Story, Mama.* New York: Orchard Books, 1989.

Joosse, Barbara M. *Mama, Do You Love Me?* San Francisco: Chronicle Books, 1991.

Kasza, Keiko. *A Mother for Choco.* New York: G. P. Putnam's Sons, 1992.

Kroll, Steven. *Happy Mother's Day.* New York: Puffin Books, 1985.

Ray, Deborah Kogan. *Stargazing Sky.* New York: Crown, 1991.

Ziefert, Harriet. *What Is Mother's Day?* New York: Harper Collins, 1992.

Zolotow, Charlotte. *This Quiet Lady.* New York: Greenwillow Books, 1992.

Music

Copus, Pamela, and Joyce Harlow. "Music of the Morning." *Holiday Story Play Music.* Plano, TX: Dreamtime Productions, P.O. Box 940061, Plano, TX 75094-0061.

FATHER'S DAY

DRAMA/PLAY EXPERIENCE

Read *Little Nino's Pizzeria* by Karen Barbour to introduce the theme of Father's Day. (See bibliography on page 165.) Nino makes the best pizza in town, with the help of his son Tony. But when Nino turns the pizzeria into a fancy restaurant, life for both changes drastically. Demonstrate the simpletees costumes and play props.

Simpletees Costumes

Use the simpletees costumes of Nino and Tony for a dramatic play experience. (See figures 10.1, 10.2, and 10.3.)

Play Props

Play props can include any restaurant props, such as a cash register, note pads, pencils, telephone, trays, aprons, plastic pizza slices, and other food.

Face Masks

Create face masks of Nino and Tony. Use tagboard templates and trace the different characters. (See figure 10.4 and 10.5.)

Stick Puppets/Paper Bag Theater

Make stick puppets of Nino and Tony. (See figure 10.6) Create a paper bag theater for the stick puppets. (See figure 1.5 on page 6.) Present the tale of Nino and Tony to a friend or take home and present to parents or guardians.

(Text continues on page 159.)

Fig. 10.1. Simpletees costumes: Father's Day.

Nino

Glue gun

XL blue, short-sleeved T-shirt

Tony

Glue gun

XL blue, short-sleeved T-shirt

Fig. 10.2. Nino and Tony bow tie directions and pattern.

Materials:

Yellow craft felt square
Scissors
Glue gun

What to Do:

Use tie patterns and trace 2 of each box shape on the yellow felt.

Cut out felt ties and glue gun pairs together in the middle.

Glue gun ties to T-shirts at the center of the neck opening.

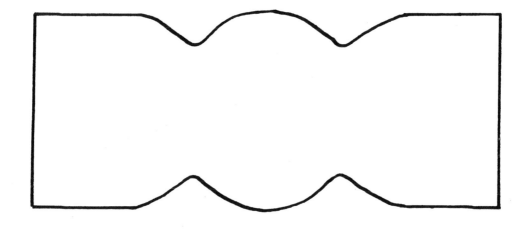

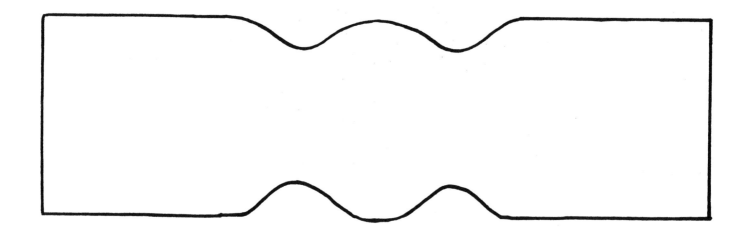

Fig. 10.3. Nino and Tony apron directions and illustrations.

Materials

⅜ yard white craft felt
Scissors
Glue gun
Permanent marker

What to Do:

Cut 2 felt rectangles 13" X 18".

Cut out apron neck opening.

Glue gun apron straps at the shoulder seams of the T-shirts.

Write Nino's and Tony's names on the aprons.

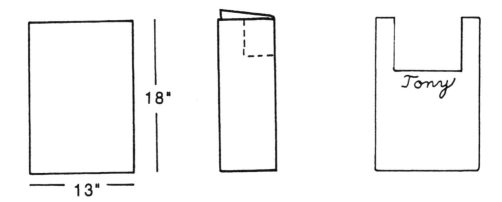

Fig. 10.4. Nino face mask pattern.

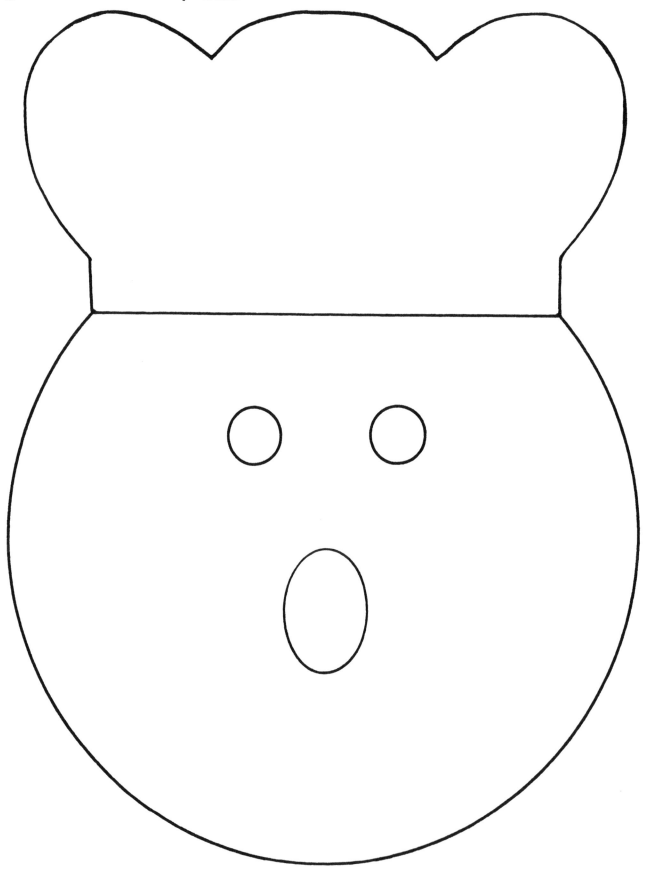

Fig. 10.5. Tony face mask pattern.

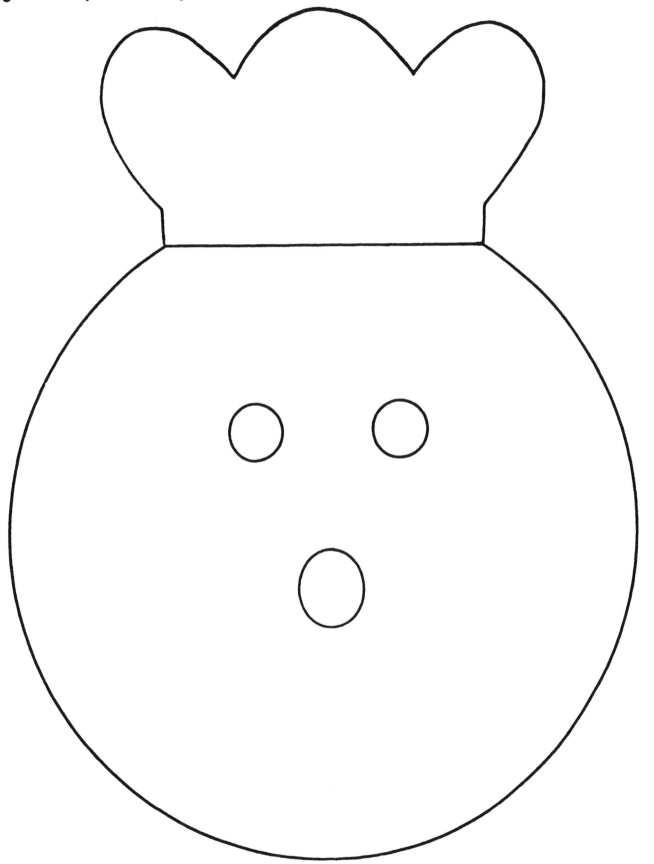

Fig. 10.6. Nino and Tony stick puppet patterns.

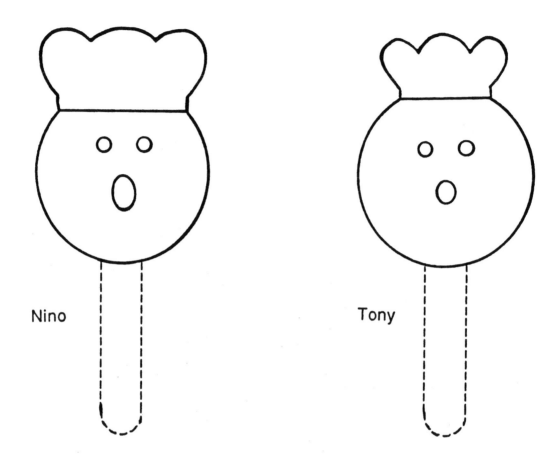

Nino

Tony

LITERATURE/WRITING EXPERIENCE

Father's Day *Versions*

Experience a variety of stories about fathers and Father's Day. For example, in *What Is Father's Day?* by Harriet Ziefert, a little mouse looks for the perfect Father's Day gift. Daddy comes home late every night, but one night he brings home a special father-and-son project in *When Daddy Comes Home* by Linda Wagner Tyler. In Robin McKinley's *My Father Is in the Navy*, a little girl does not remember her father because his job takes him away from home. And Baby Tiger is lost and looking for his daddy in *Are You My Daddy?* by Carla Dijs. (See bibliography on page 165.)

Father's Day *Children's Version*

Write a children's version about Father's Day on a large sheet of chart paper.

Key-Word Books and Key Words

Make a key-word book with the unique or important words from *Little Nino's Pizzeria* by Karen Barbour. (See bibliography on page 165.) The key words for *Little Nino's Pizzeria* are as follows:

Little	Nino	Tony
dad	pizza	dough
sauce	cheese	customers
restaurant		

Chef's Hat Shape Book

Make a chef's hat shape book by tracing the chef's hat shape from a tagboard template. (See figure 10.7.) Illustrate the book and write a story or dictate it to the teacher. Use the key words for an independent writing experience.

I Love My Daddy Because

In *I Love My Daddy Because...*, Laurel Porter-Gaylord shows animal fathers caring for their young. (See bibliography on page 165.) Write or dictate a sentence to the teacher to tell why your dad or other trusted male adult is special. Draw a picture to illustrate the sentence.

Weird Parents

A boy has weird parents who do weird things that embarrass him in *Weird Parents* by Audrey Wood. (See bibliography on page 165.) What do your parents or guardians do that is different or embarrassing? Write the responses on a piece of chart paper.

Fig. 10.7. Chef's hat shape book directions and pattern.

Materials:

White construction paper
Tagboard
White paper
Scissors
Stapler
Markers or pencils
Key words

What to Do:

Make a tagboard template from the pattern.

Trace and cut out 2 hat shapes from construction paper.

Teacher may precut white pages.

Staple the cover and white pages together.

Illustrate the book and write or dictate the story.

Use key words for an independent writing experience.

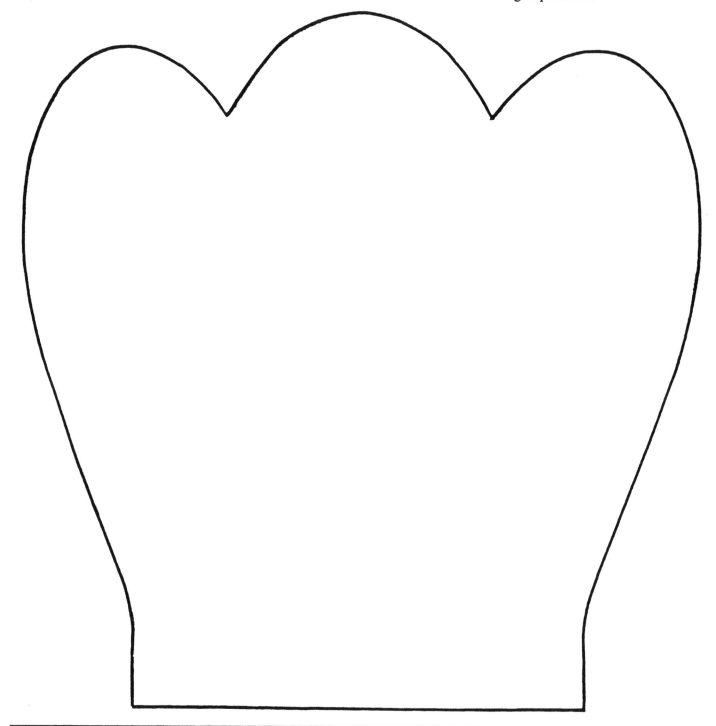

COOPERATIVE/GROUP EXPERIENCE

If You Get Lost Map

Paul and Carol try to outdo each other in losing and finding their father in *What If Dad Gets Lost at the Zoo?* by Ginette Lamont Clarke and Florence Stevens. (See bibliography on page 165.) Make a map to show dads and other trusted adults how to find their way around at the zoo.

Build a Parent Trap

Ann decides to catch and keep a grown-up for a pet in *The Grown-up Trap* by Ib Spang Olsen. (See bibliography on page 165.) Make a parent trap by using crêpe-paper streamers to weave throughout the classroom or outside using trees and fences.

ART/CRAFT EXPERIENCE

Tempera Painting

Read *First Pink Light* by Eloise Greenfield. (See bibliography on page 165.) Tyree's father has been away taking care of Grandma and will be coming home in the morning—at the first pink light. Use a red tempera cake and water to paint a thin transparent layer on a piece of paper. This thin layer of tempera will give a pink appearance. After the paint has dried, use markers to draw a picture of your dad, grandfather, or other trusted adult. Write a caption for the painting. Display the paintings on the walls or the bulletin board. Bind together to make a class book.

My Father

A father's dreams come true for his youngest daughter in *My Father* by Judy Collins. (See bibliography on page 165.) Draw a picture to illustrate a dream or promise that your father, grandfather, or some other trusted adult has made to you.

Father's Day Present

A little mouse looks for the perfect gift for her father in *What Is Father's Day?* by Harriet Ziefert. (See bibliography on page 165.) Find a large, smooth stone to make a paperweight for your dad, grandfather, or other trusted adult. Wash and dry the stone. Use poster paint and paint a design on the stone. Place the stone on waxed paper. When the design is dry, paint a thin layer of white glue over the stone and let it dry.

COOKING/MATH EXPERIENCE

Thumb Print Cookies

In *Farm Morning* by David McPhail, a father feeds all the animals on the farm, with the help of his daughter, before realizing that they have not had breakfast. (See bibliography on page 165.) Make thumb print cookies by following the recipe in figure 10.8.

Snack for Father's Day

Corey's father makes the best spaghetti, dresses like Batman, and pretends to be a dog in *Daddy Makes the Best Spaghetti* by Anna Grossnickle Hines. (See bibliography on page 165.) Make a Father's Day snack by filling a small decorated lunch bag with popcorn or granola.

SCIENCE/DISCOVERY EXPERIENCE

Discovery Museum

Create a discovery museum to display photographs of fathers or male relatives. Have the children bring photographs of their fathers, guardians, or grandfathers from home. Display the photographs on a bulletin board in the classroom. Explore the photographs with a group or individually.

Robots

In *The Trouble with Dad* by Babette Cole, Dad's robots create many adventures for his family. (See bibliography on page 165.) Make a robot by using a big box for a base. Use empty paper tubes and other throw-away items to add to the base. Make individual robots or build one as a group activity.

Soaps

Make colored soaps for Father's Day presents. Mix 2 cups of white soap flakes with ½ cup water that has been tinted with food coloring. Form the mixture into balls or other shapes. Allow the soap to dry on waxed paper for several days. Wrap the soaps in tissue paper and give to your special dad or relative.

Fig. 10.8. Thumb print cookies recipe.

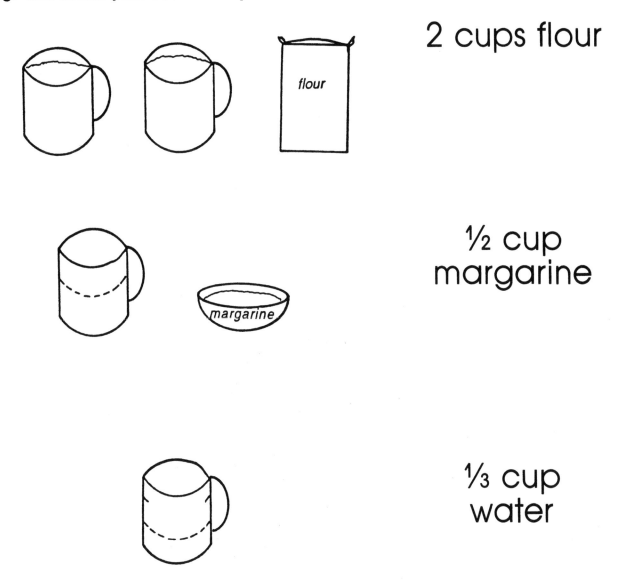

2 cups flour

½ cup margarine

⅓ cup water

Mix ingredients into a stiff ball. Roll 1 teaspoon dough into a ball on wax paper. Press thumb into ball. Place on cookie sheet and bake at 350⁰ for 8 to 10 minutes. Fill thumb prints with honey.

MUSIC/GAME EXPERIENCE

Moonhorse and Me

When Dad falls asleep on the front porch, a young girl goes on an adventure among the stars in *Moonhorse* by Mary Pope Osborne. (See bibliography on page 165.) Make a moon wand. (See figure 10.9.) Listen to the music "Moonhorse" by Pamela Copus and Joyce Harlow in *Holiday Story Play Music*. (See bibliography on page 165.) Pretend to fly on a moonhorse. Move your arms to the music and wave your moon wand.

Fig. 10.9. Moon wand directions and pattern.

Materials:

Tagboard
Yellow construction paper
Scissors
Ribbon streamers
Tape or glue
Drinking straws

What to Do:

Using a tagboard moon template, trace and cut out moon shapes from construction paper.

Tape or glue ribbon streamers to the moon.

Tape or glue the moon to a drinking straw to make a wand.

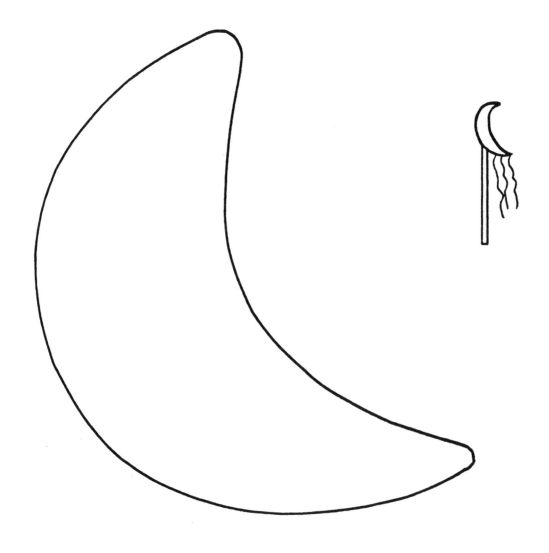

BIBLIOGRAPHY

Barbour, Karen. *Little Nino's Pizzeria*. San Diego, CA: Harcourt Brace Jovanovich, 1987.

Clarke, Ginette Lamont, and Florence Stevens. *What If Dad Gets Lost at the Zoo?* Plattsburgh, NY: Tundra Books, 1991.

Cole, Babette. *The Trouble with Dad*. New York: G. P. Putnam's Sons, 1985.

Collins, Judy. *My Father*. Boston: Little, Brown, 1989.

Dijs, Carla. *Are You My Daddy?* New York: Simon & Schuster, 1990.

Greenfield, Eloise. *First Pink Light*. New York: Writers & Readers, 1991.

Hines, Anna Grossnickle. *Daddy Makes the Best Spaghetti*. New York: Clarion Books, 1986.

McKinley, Robin. *My Father Is in the Navy*. New York: Greenwillow Books, 1992.

McPhail, David. *Farm Morning*. San Diego, CA: Harcourt Brace Jovanovich, 1985.

Olsen, Ib Spang. *The Grown-up Trap*. Charlottesville, VA: Thomasson-Grant, 1990.

Osborne, Mary Pope. *Moonhorse*. New York: Alfred A. Knopf, 1991.

Porter-Gaylord, Laurel. *I Love My Daddy Because...* New York: Dutton Children's Books, 1991.

Tyler, Linda Wagner. *When Daddy Comes Home*. New York: Puffin Books, 1986.

Wood, Audrey. *Weird Parents*. New York: Dial Books for Young Readers, 1990.

Ziefert, Harriet. *What Is Father's Day?* New York: Harper Collins, 1992.

Music

Copus, Pamela, and Joyce Harlow. "Moonhorse." *Holiday Story Play Music*. Plano, TX: Dreamtime Productions, P.O. Box 940061, Plano, TX 75094-0061.

CHAPTER 11

FOURTH OF JULY

DRAMA/PLAY EXPERIENCE

Read *Watch the Stars Come Out* by Riki Levinson to introduce the theme of Fourth of July. (See bibliography on page 178.) After 23 days on a big boat, a red-haired girl and her brother sail past the Statue of Liberty and begin a new life in America with their mother, father, and sister. Demonstrate the simpletees costumes and play props.

Simpletees Costumes

Use simpletees costumes of the red-haired girl and the brother for a dramatic play experience. (See figure 11.1, in addition to figure 3.2 on page 38.)

Play Props

Play props can include a table and chairs, a picnic basket, plastic food, and a nurse's or doctor's kit.

Face Masks

Create face masks of the red-haired girl and the brother. Use tagboard templates and trace the patterns. Illustrate the masks with facial features for the various characters. (See figure 11.2 and 11.3.)

Stick Puppets/Paper Bag Theater

Make stick puppets of the red-haired girl and the brother. (See figure 11.4.) Create a paper bag theater for the stick puppets and present the story of *Watch the Stars Come Out* by Riki Levinson to a friend or parents. (See figure 1.5 on page 6.)

(Text continues on page 171.)

Fig. 11.1. Simpletees costumes: Fourth of July.

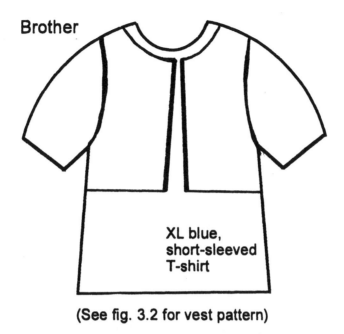

Brother

XL blue,
short-sleeved
T-shirt

(See fig. 3.2 for vest pattern)

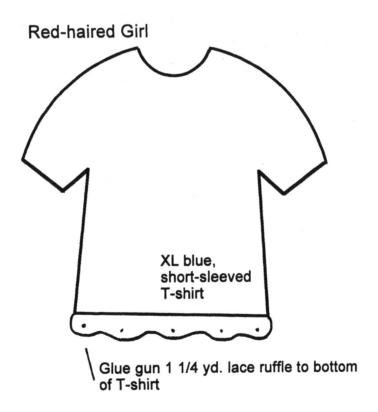

Red-haired Girl

XL blue,
short-sleeved
T-shirt

Glue gun 1 1/4 yd. lace ruffle to bottom
of T-shirt

Fig. 11.2. Red-haired girl face mask pattern.

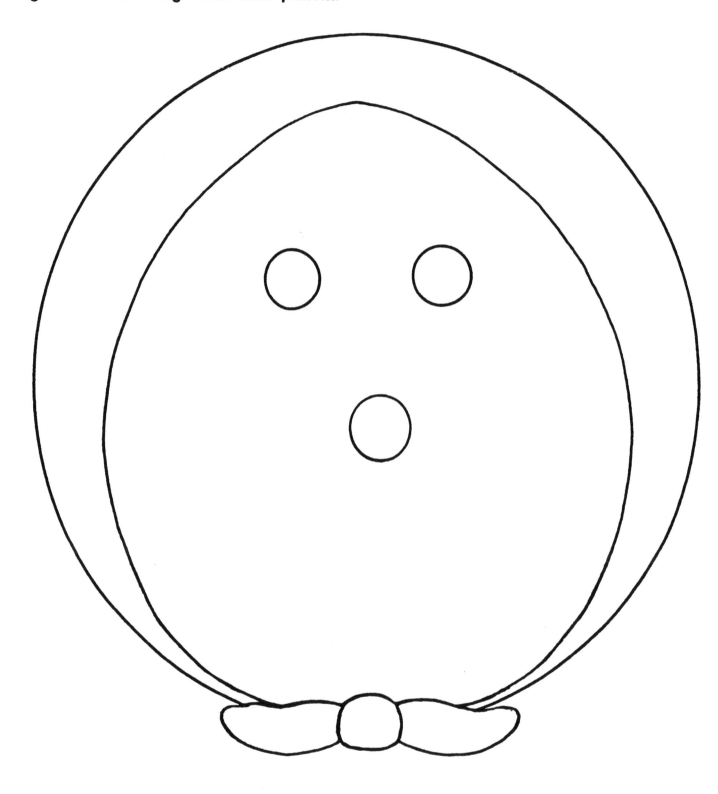

Fig. 11.3. Brother face mask pattern.

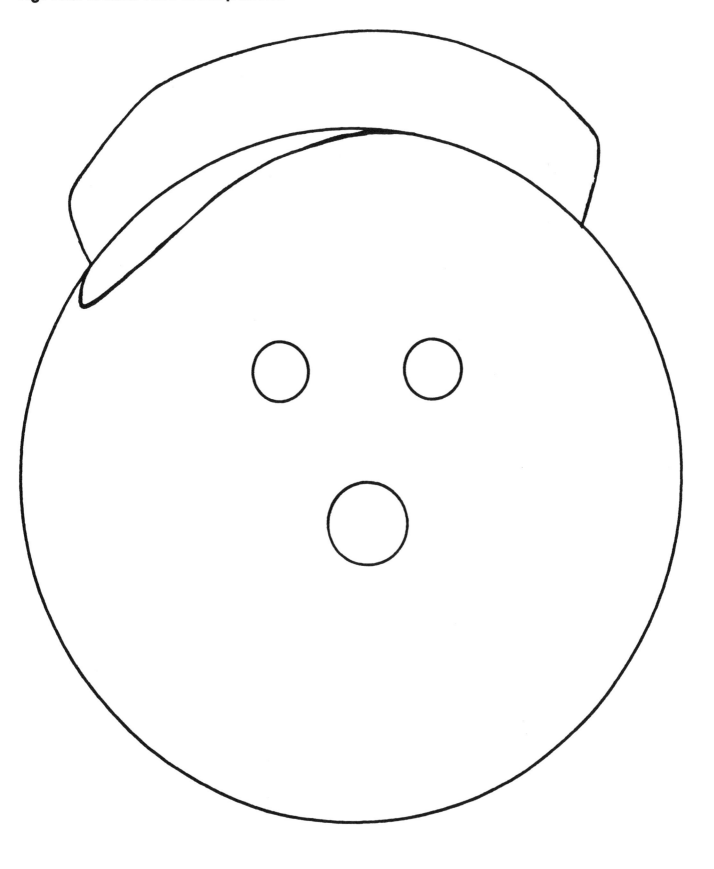

Fig. 11.4. Fourth of July stick puppet patterns.

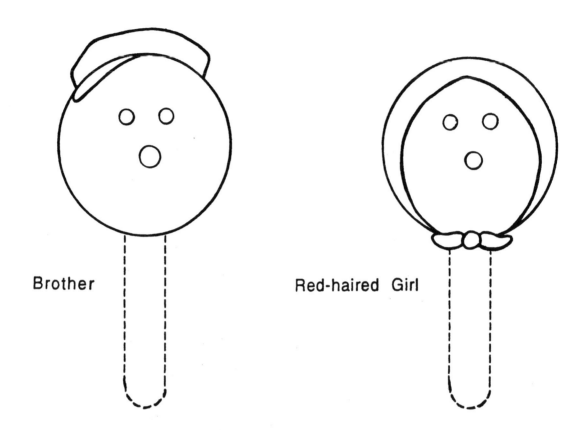

Brother

Red-haired Girl

LITERATURE/WRITING EXPERIENCE

Fourth of July *Versions*

Read a variety of stories about the Fourth of July and America. For example, *Hurray for the Fourth of July* by Wendy Watson is the story of a small-town family's patriotic celebration. Alice Dalgliesh's *The Fourth of July Story* retells the story of the signing of the Declaration of Independence. *I Hear America Singing* by Walt Whitman celebrates the American spirit. (See bibliography on page 178.)

Fourth of July *Children's Version*

After sharing the different stories about America and the Fourth of July, write a children's version on a large sheet of chart paper.

Key-Word Books and Key Words

Make a key-word book with the unique or important words from the book *Watch the Stars Come Out* by Riki Levinson. (See bibliography on page 178.) The key words for *Watch the Stars Come Out* are as follows:

watch	stars	brother
sister	grandma	Mama
Papa	America	boat
statue		

Liberty Shape Book

Make a Liberty shape book by tracing the Liberty shape from a tagboard template. (See figure 11.5.) Illustrate and write a story about the red-haired girl and her brother or dictate it to the teacher. Use the key words for an independent writing experience.

ABC America

In *Oscar de Mejo's ABC* by Oscar de Mejo, American myths and legends are used to illustrate the letters of the alphabet. (See bibliography on page 178.) Create an ABC book about America as you know it.

Fig. 11.5. Liberty shape book directions and pattern.

Materials:

Grey construction paper
Tagboard
White paper
Scissors
Stapler
Markers or pencils
Key words

What to Do:

Make a tagboard template from the pattern.

Trace and cut out 2 Liberty shapes from construction paper.

Teacher may precut white pages.

Staple the cover and white pages together.

Illustrate the book and write or dictate the story.

Use key words for an independent writing experience.

COOPERATIVE/GROUP EXPERIENCE

Lemon to Lemonade

Follow the process of turning lemons into lemonade by reading Ali Mitgutsch's *From Lemon to Lemonade*. (See bibliography on page 178.) Create a lemonade stand or factory. Use lemon squeezers and make fresh lemonade.

People Mural

Americans come from a variety of races, heritages, and cultures. Read *People, People, Everywhere!* by Nancy Van Laan and Peter Spier's *People* and experience the diversity of America. (See bibliography on page 178.) Make a people mural by using people colors and other assorted tempera paints. Fill the paper with people.

ART/CRAFT EXPERIENCE

Tempera Painting

Paint a tempera picture of the red-haired girl and her brother from *Watch the Stars Come Out* by Riki Levinson. (See bibliography on page 178.) Use red, blue, brown, and people-color tempera. Write or dictate a sentence or story about the picture. Display the paintings on the walls or the bulletin board. Bind the paintings together to make a class book.

Flags

Peter Spier's *The Star-Spangled Banner* illustrates the American national anthem and celebrates the American flag. (See bibliography on page 178.) Create your own flag by using red and blue tempera or markers on white paper.

Sidewalk Art

Make sidewalk chalk by mixing red, white, and blue tempera paint with plaster of paris. Pour the mixture into a mold and let it dry. Use the chalk to decorate sidewalks with a patriotic theme.

Statue of Liberty Crown

The Story of the Statue of Liberty by Betsy Maestro and Giulio Maestro is the history of the symbol that greeted millions of immigrants to America. (See bibliography on page 178.) Make a crown similar to the Statue of Liberty's by folding a paper plate in half and cutting it. (See figure 11.6.) Open the plate and bend the points upward to make the crown. Put gummed stars on the points and wear the crown in a Fourth of July parade.

Fig. 11.6. Liberty Crown directions and illustration.

Materials:

9" paper plates
Scissors
Gummed stars
Markers

What to Do:

Fold paper plate in half.

Cut wedges from the center point on the fold to within 1" of the rim of the plate.

Fold back points to make a Liberty crown.

Decorate with markers and stars.

Firecrackers

Firecrackers are a traditional part of Fourth of July celebrations. Make a firecracker by wrapping an empty cardboard tube with a piece of 9-by-12-inch red, white, or blue tissue paper. Tie the ends with curling ribbon and decorate the tube with flag or star stickers.

COOKING/MATH EXPERIENCE

Dried Fruit

The long ocean journey to America described in *Watch the Stars Come Out*, by Riki Levinson, required provisions that would not spoil. (See bibliography on page 178.) Taste a variety of dried fruits, such as apples, raisins, and apricots.

Birthday Cookies

Read *The Fourth of July Story* by Alice Dalgliesh to discover the meaning behind the Independence Day celebration. (See bibliography on page 178.) Celebrate America's birthday by making birthday cookies. (See figure 11.7.)

Fourth of July Picnic

Hurray for the Fourth of July by Wendy Watson illustrates the fun of a picnic lunch on Independence Day. (See bibliography on page 178.) Celebrate the Fourth of July with a picnic that includes hot dogs, popcorn, and ice cream.

Fig. 11.7. Birthday cookies recipe.

½ cup
peanut butter

½ cup honey

½ cup cocoa

1 cup wheat germ

Combine ingredients and roll into small balls. Roll the balls in confectioner's sugar and place in the refrigerator for 2 to 3 hours.

SCIENCE/DISCOVERY EXPERIENCE

Discovery Museum

Create a discovery museum to display items and books about America and the Fourth of July. Display the collections and contributions on a table, shelf, or counter top in the classroom. Label the items with sentence strips. Explore the objects with a group or individually.

Quill Pen Writing

John Hancock loved to sign his name, and his signature on the Declaration of Independence was so large that King George didn't need his glass to see it. That's part of the story in *Will You Sign Here, John Hancock?* by Jean Fritz. (See bibliography on page 178.) Use a quill and ink just as John Hancock did. Make a quill pen by cutting the end of a feather at an angle. Make ink by mixing ½ cup berry juice with ½ teaspoon of salt and ½ teaspoon of vinegar.

MUSIC/GAME EXPERIENCE

Yankee Doodle

Celebrate the Fourth of July with a choral reading or singing of "Yankee Doodle":

> Oh, Yankee Doodle went to town
>
> a-riding on a pony,
>
> He stuck a feather in his cap
>
> and called it macaroni.
>
> Yankee Doodle, keep it up,
>
> Yankee Doodle Dandy,
>
> Mind the music and the step
>
> and with the girls be handy.

People Parade

Harriet Ziefert's *Parade* describes the rhythmic sounds, colorful sights, and delightful smells associated with parades. (See bibliography on page 178.) Listen to "People Parade" by Pamela Copus and Joyce Harlow in *Holiday Story Play Music* and celebrate the Fourth of July with a parade. (See bibliography on page 178.) Use existing rhythm instruments or make your own. Create parade floats by decorating shoe boxes with red, white, and blue crêpe-paper streamers. March in the Fourth of July parade while playing "Parade," performed by Pamela Copus, or other good parade music.

BIBLIOGRAPHY

Dalgliesh, Alice. *The Fourth of July Story*. New York: Aladdin Books, 1956.

de Mejo, Oscar. *Oscar de Mejo's ABC*. New York: Harper Collins, 1992.

Fritz, Jean. *Will You Sign Here, John Hancock?* New York: Coward-McCann, 1976.

Levinson, Riki. *Watch the Stars Come Out*. New York: E. P. Dutton, 1985.

Maestro, Betsy, and Giulio Maestro. *The Story of the Statue of Liberty*. New York: Mulberry Books, 1986.

Mitgutsch, Ali. *From Lemon to Lemonade*. Minneapolis, MN: Carolrhoda Books, 1986.

Spier, Peter. *People*. New York: Doubleday, 1980.

_____. *The Star-Spangled Banner*. New York: Doubleday, 1973.

Van Laan, Nancy. *People, People, Everywhere!* New York: Alfred A. Knopf, 1992.

Watson, Wendy. *Hurray for the Fourth of July*. New York: Clarion Books, 1992.

Whitman, Walt. *I Hear America Singing*. New York: Philomel Books, 1991.

Ziefert, Harriet. *Parade*. New York: Bantam Books, 1990.

Music

Copus, Pamela, and Joyce Harlow. "People Parade." *Holiday Story Play Music*. Plano, TX: Dreamtime Productions, P.O. Box 940061, Plano, TX 75094-0061.

CHAPTER 12

AVIATION DAY

DRAMA/PLAY EXPERIENCE

Read *The Wing Shop* by Elvira Woodruff to introduce the theme of Aviation Day. (See bibliography on page 198.) Matthew does not like his new home on Finley Street, but he is too young to drive or take the bus back to his old house on Main Street. One day Matthew discovers Lucy and The Wing Shop and finds an airborne way to get back home. Demonstrate the simpletees costumes and play props.

Simpletees Costumes

Use the simpletees costumes of Matthew and Lucy for a dramatic play experience. (See figure 12.1.)

Play Props

Play props can include plastic airplanes, scarves, and goggles. Have a wing shop and make sets of felt wings, such as seagull wings, bat wings, and airplane wings. (See figures 12.2, 12.3, and 12.4.)

Face Masks

Create face masks of Matthew and Lucy. Use tagboard templates and trace the patterns. Illustrate the masks with facial features for the various characters. (See figures 12.5 and 12.6.)

Stick Puppets/Paper Bag Theater

Make stick puppets of Matthew and Lucy. (See figure 12.7.) Create a paper bag theater for the stick puppets and present the story of Matthew and Lucy to a friend or families. (See figure 1.5 on page 6.)

(Text continues on page 187.)

Fig. 12.1. Simpletees costumes: Aviation Day.

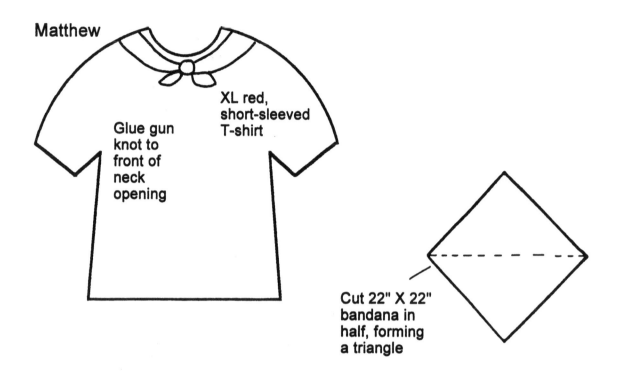

Matthew

Glue gun knot to front of neck opening

XL red, short-sleeved T-shirt

Cut 22" X 22" bandana in half, forming a triangle

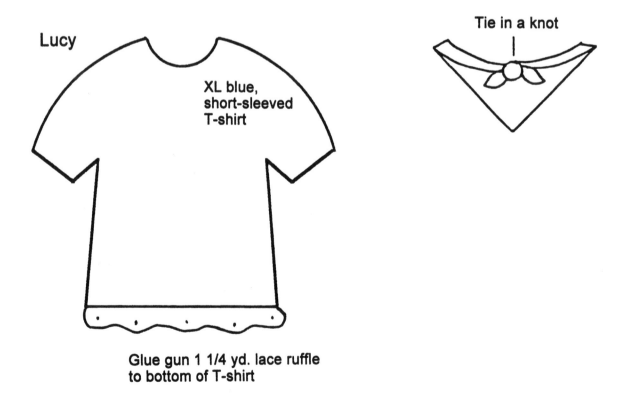

Lucy

XL blue, short-sleeved T-shirt

Tie in a knot

Glue gun 1 1/4 yd. lace ruffle to bottom of T-shirt

Fig. 12.2. Seagull wings directions and pattern.

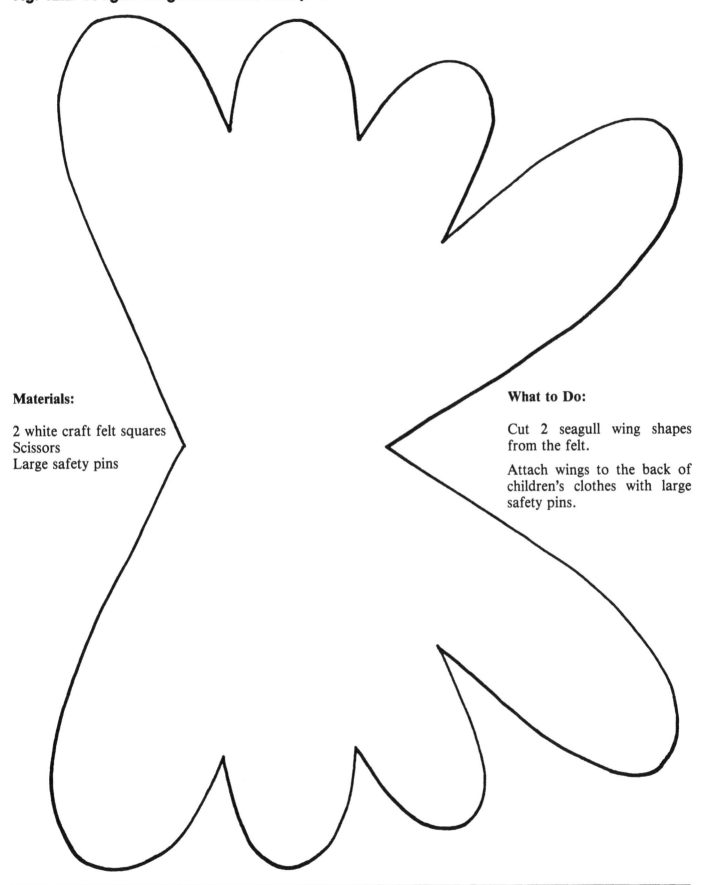

Materials:

2 white craft felt squares
Scissors
Large safety pins

What to Do:

Cut 2 seagull wing shapes from the felt.

Attach wings to the back of children's clothes with large safety pins.

Fig. 12.3. Bat wings directions and pattern.

Materials:

2 black craft felt
   squares
Scissors
Large safety pins

What to Do:

Cut 2 bat wing shapes from
the felt.

Attach wings to the back of
children's clothes with large
safety pins.

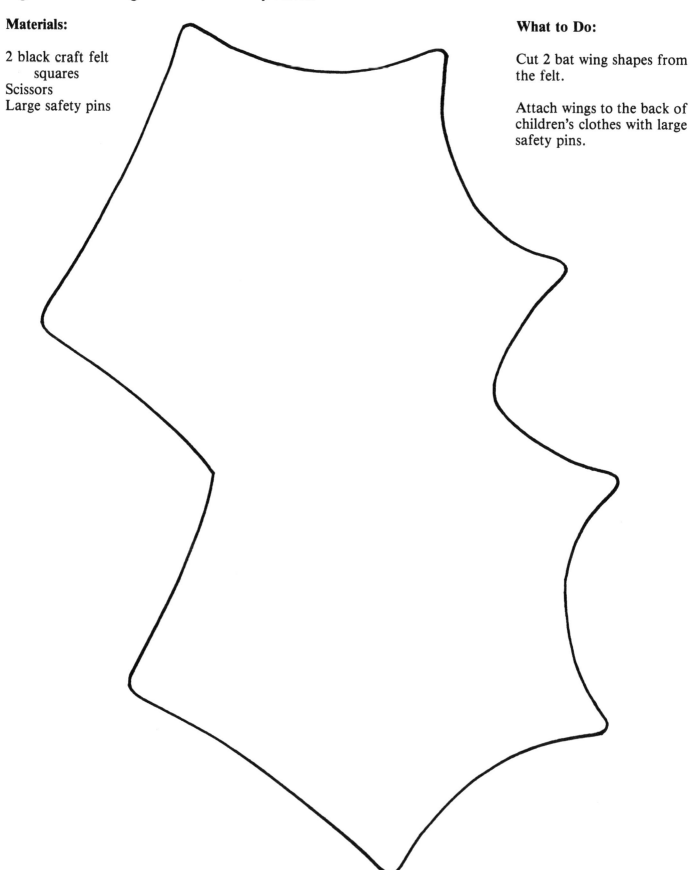

Fig. 12.4. Airplane wings directions and pattern.

Materials:

2 blue craft felt
    squares
Scissors
Large safety pins

What to Do:

Cut 2 airplane shapes from the felt.

Attach wings to the back of children's clothes with large safety pins.

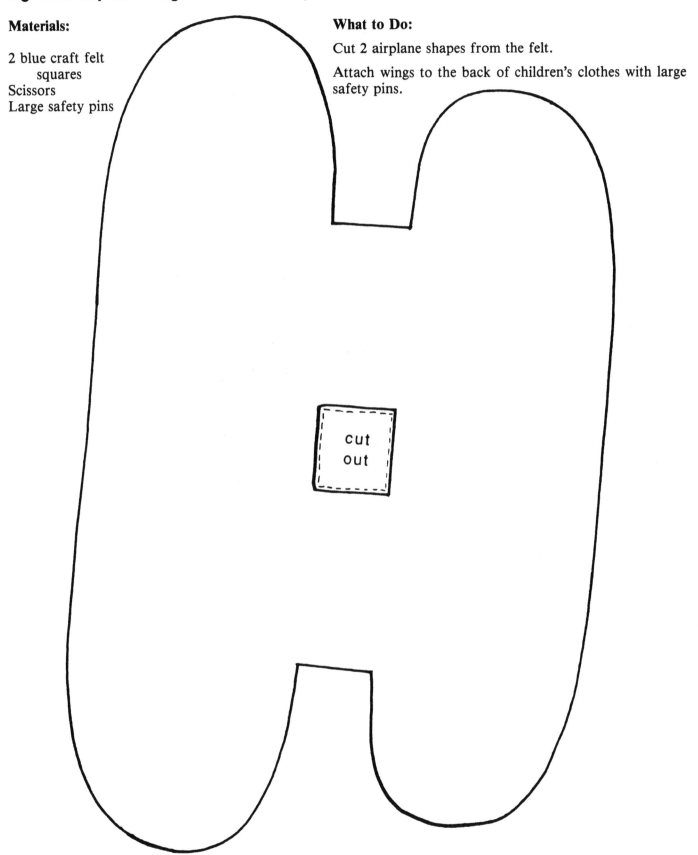

cut
out

Fig. 12.5. Matthew face mask pattern.

Fig. 12.6. Lucy face mask pattern.

Fig. 12.7. Aviation Day stick puppet patterns.

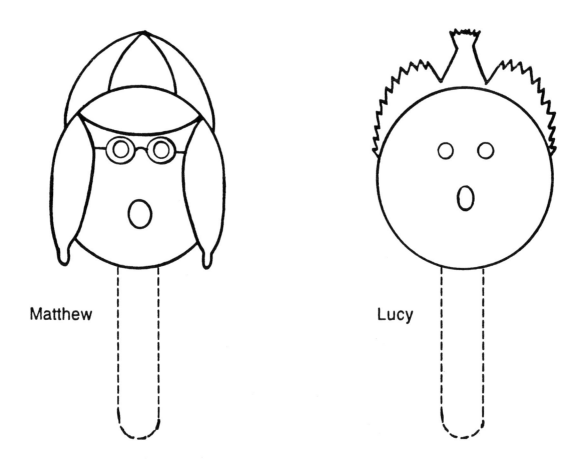

Matthew　　　　　　　　　Lucy

LITERATURE/WRITING EXPERIENCE

Aviation Day *Versions*

Experience a variety of books about aviation. For example, *Flying* by Gail Gibbons describes the history of flight from passenger balloons to the space shuttle. Alice Provensen and Martin Provensen's *The Glorious Flight: Across the Channel with Louis Bleriot* is the story of the pioneer aviator. *Flight* by Robert Burleigh tells the story of Charles Lindbergh's 33½ hour flight from Long Island to Paris in 1927. *Planes* by Anne Rockwell is a basic introduction to aviation. (See bibliography on pages 197-98.)

Aviation Day *Children's Version*

Write a children's version about aviation on a large sheet of chart paper.

Key-Word Books and Key Words

Make a key-word book with the unique or important words from *The Wing Shop* by Elvira Woodruff. (See bibliography on page 198.) The key words for *The Wing Shop* are as follows:

Matthew	Lucy	wings
fly	shop	move
Main Street	Finley Street	different
neighborhood		

Balloon Shape Book

Read *Hot-Air Henry* by Mary Calhoun. Henry is a Siamese cat who stows away in a hot-air balloon. (See bibliography on page 197.) Make a balloon shape book by tracing the balloon shape from a tagboard template. (See figure 12.8.) Illustrate the book and write a story or dictate it to the teacher. Use the key words for an independent writing experience.

Fig. 12.8. Hot-air balloon shape book directions and pattern.

Materials:

Blue construction paper
Tagboard
White paper
Scissors
Stapler
Markers or
    pencils
Key words

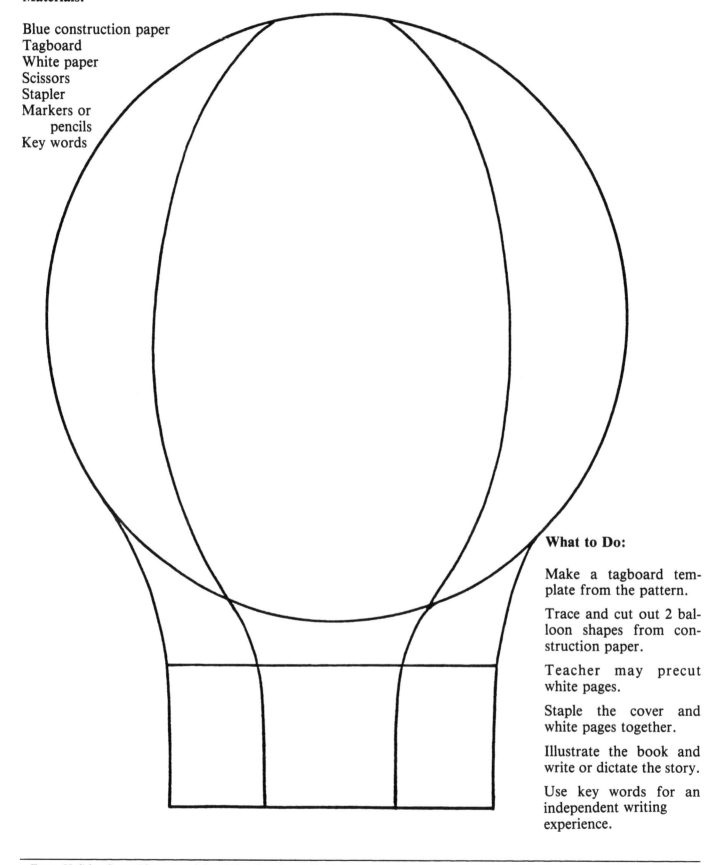

What to Do:

Make a tagboard template from the pattern.

Trace and cut out 2 balloon shapes from construction paper.

Teacher may precut white pages.

Staple the cover and white pages together.

Illustrate the book and write or dictate the story.

Use key words for an independent writing experience.

My Little Suitcase

Read *Maebelle's Suitcase* by Tricia Tusa. (See bibliography on page 198.) Maebelle's bird-friend Binkle borrows a suitcase to use when he heads south for the winter. When the suitcase proves to be too heavy, Maebelle finds the solution to her friend's dilemma. Pack a suitcase for your travels. Cut out pictures from magazines and catalogs to show what you would take on your flight. (See figure 12.9.)

Butterfly Wishes

Read *I Wish I Were a Butterfly* by James Howe. (See bibliography on page 197.) A little cricket wishes that he were a butterfly because the frog told him he was ugly. Make a butterfly wish book. Give each child a paper butterfly shape. (See figure 12.10.) Complete the sentence, "I wish I were a _____ because _____." Illustrate your wish and combine the butterflies to make a class book.

Storytelling

Emily and the Crows by Elaine Greenstein is the delightful tale of a little girl who makes herself crow wings so she can find out what Emily the cow has to say. (See bibliography on page 197.) Make up a story to share with the rest of the group.

Fig. 12.9. My little suitcase directions and pattern. (Continued on page 190.)

Materials:	What to Do:
Construction paper (9" X 12") Tagboard	Fold construction paper in half.
Markers or pencils Scissors	Place tagboard suitcase template on the fold of the paper and trace the shape.
Catalogs Glue stick	Cut out suitcase and draw or glue articles cut from catalogs inside.

Fig. 12.9. My little suitcase directions and pattern.

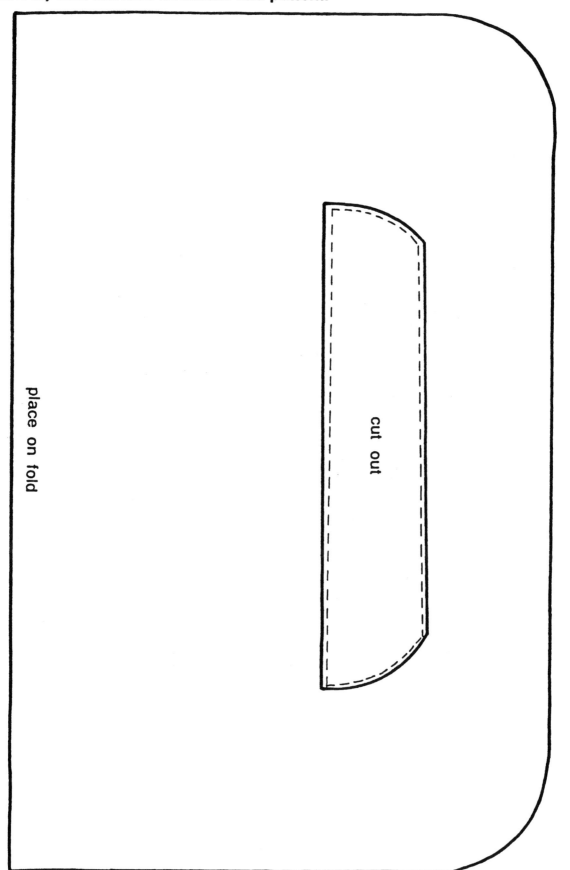

place on fold

cut out

Fig. 12.10. Butterfly wings pattern.

COOPERATIVE/GROUP EXPERIENCE

Skykites

In *Simon and the Wind* by Gilles Tibo, Simon wants to fly like the wind, but decides that it is easier to make other things fly instead. (See bibliography on page 198.) Use paper bags and make skykites to fly on a windy day. (See figure 12.11.)

Fig. 12.11. Skykite directions and illustration.

Materials:

8½" X 11" regular-weight paper
Hole punch
Markers or crayons
Kite string

What to Do:

Fold down 1" on long side of paper.

Fold in half with flap inside.

Punch one hole in the middle of each folded-down flap.

Decorate with markers or crayons.

Tie a 20" kite string through the holes with loose knots, forming a V shape.

Tie another 24" string to the V-shaped string.

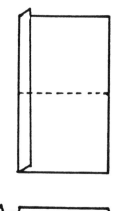

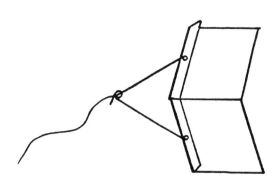

U.F.O. Spaceships

Read "U.F.O." in *Machine Poems* by Jill Bennett. (See bibliography on page 197.) Create a U.F.O. spaceship by using a large box as a base and adding parts from recycled throw-aways, such as egg cartons, berry baskets, paper tubes, and so forth. Use fluorescent paint and paint the spaceship in futuristic colors.

Amelia's Fantastic Flight

Amelia loves airplanes, so she decides to build one. She then sets off for a journey around the world in *Amelia's Fantastic Flight* by Rose Bursik. (See bibliography on page 197.) Make a wall mural of the places or countries the class would like to visit.

ART/CRAFT EXPERIENCE

Tempera Painting

Paint a tempera picture of Matthew and his wings from *The Wing Shop* by Elvira Woodruff. (See bibliography on page 198.) Use white, blue, pink, green, and people-color tempera. Write or dictate a sentence or story about the picture. Display the paintings on the walls or the bulletin board. Bind the paintings together to make a class book.

Wing-A-Dings

In *Wing-A-Ding* by Lynn Littlefield Hoopes, a favorite toy gets stuck in a tree, so a young boy and his friends try everything to get it down. (See bibliography on page 197.) Make your own wing-a-ding and watch out for the trees when flying it outside. (See figure 12.12.)

Fig. 12.12. Wing-a-dings directions and illustration.

Materials:	What to Do:
9" paper plates	Cut out center of paper plates.
Stapler	
Markers	Staple 2 paper plate rim-rings together.
	Decorate with markers.

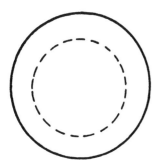 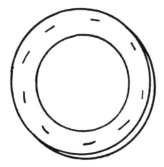 

A Pair of Wings

Read *If All the World Were Paper* by Miriam Nerlove. (See bibliography on page 198.) A little boy paints himself a huge pair of wings that cannot be bought. Discuss where you would go if you had a pair of wings. Use 18-by-24-inch white drawing paper or other large paper to make wings. Lie flat on the floor on top of the paper and have a friend or teacher trace across the tops of your arms. Draw a wing shape, using the top line for the starting point. Decorate the wings or leave them white. Use a large safety pin to secure the wings to the back of your clothing. Use masking tape and attach the wings to your wrists. Take a walk using the wings.

Leonardo da Vinci

Read *Leonardo da Vinci* by Alice Provensen and Martin Provensen and Ibi Lepscky's *Leonardo da Vinci* to find out about the inventor's experiments with flight. (See bibliography on pages 197-98.) Use pencils and make sketches of your own idea for a flying machine.

COOKING/MATH EXPERIENCE

Airplane Snacks

Explore the inside of an airliner and other aspects of aviation in Gallimard Jeunesse's *Airplanes and Flying Machines.* Have an airplane snack by serving crackers, cubes of cheese, and peanuts in television or microwave dinner trays. Select flight attendants to serve the snacks to the other passengers.

Outer Space Treats

Celebrate Aviation Day with an outer space treat. Place prepared pudding in sealed plastic bags. Leave an opening in the bag so that the pudding can be squeezed through. Pretend to be on a space walk while enjoying the pudding.

Space Balls

Make space balls to enjoy while experiencing the aviation activities by following the recipe in figure 12.13.

Fig. 12.13. Space balls recipe.

½ cup
peanut butter

1 tablespoon honey

½ cup
dry milk

roll into balls,
refrigerate 1 hour,
and eat

SCIENCE/DISCOVERY EXPERIENCE

Discovery Museum

Create a discovery museum to display items about aviation. Have children contribute a variety of flying things, such as miniature airplanes, flying insects, photographs of birds, and mobiles, kites, pinwheels, and other toys that work in the air. *Wings: A Pop-Up Book of Things That Really Fly* by Nick Bantock and Barbara Taylor's *Up, Up and Away: The Science of Flight* offer insight into the scientific aspects of flight and can also be displayed in the museum. (See bibliography on pages 197-98.) Display the items on a table, shelf, or counter top in the classroom. Use sentence strips to label the items. Explore the museum with the group or individually.

Flying Machine

Take an imaginary journey in *The Paper Airplane* by Fulvio Testa. (See bibliography on page 198.) Make a flying machine for your very own adventure. (See figure 12.14.)

Fig. 12.14. Flying machine directions and illustration.

Materials:	What to Do:
Paper plates Tape Markers	Fold paper plate in half.
	Open and fold down two flaps.
	Fold in half again with flaps inside.
	Open and fold out and down the flaps to create a paper airplane.
	Tape across the top of the flaps.
	Decorate with markers.

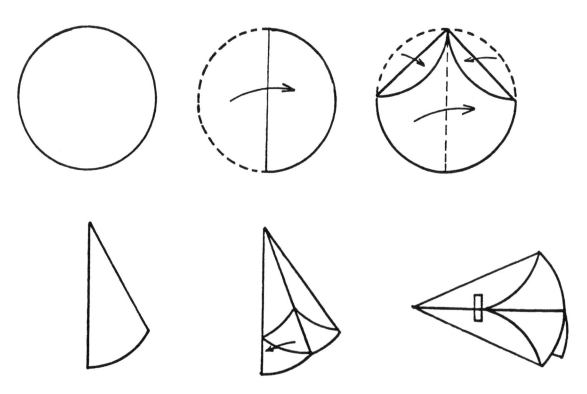

MUSIC/GAME EXPERIENCE

Wings

Wings by Jane Yolen is a retelling of the Greek legend of Daedalus and Icarus. (See bibliography on page 198.) Daedalus and Icarus escape from their tower prison by using wings, but they must be careful not to fly too close to the water, too high into the heavens, or too close to the sun. Listen to "Wings" by Pamela Copus and Joyce Harlow in *Holiday Story Play Music* or other music that simulates flight. (See bibliography on page 198.) Pretend to fly while using imaginary wings.

Star Catching

In this outdoor tag game, four or five children are star catchers, while the others are the stars. The catchers chant: "Star light, star bright, how many stars can I catch tonight?" The stars then begin to run and the catchers try to tag them. The game continues until all the stars are caught. New catchers can then be selected for the next round of star catching.

Feather Racing

Celebrate Aviation Day with a feather race similar to the game in Phil Wiswell's *Kids' Games*. Use feathers, paper plates, designated start and finish lines, and teams of four or five members to feather race. Place a paper plate with a feather on it in front of each team at the starting line. Each team member must race to the finish line and return to the starting line while carrying the feather on the plate. However, if the feather falls to the ground the team member must return to the starting line and try again.

BIBLIOGRAPHY

Bantock, Nick. *Wings: A Pop-Up Book of Things That Really Fly*. Los Angeles: Random House, 1991.

Bennett, Jill. *Machine Poems*. Oxford and New York: Oxford University Press, 1991.

Burleigh, Robert. *Flight*. New York: Philomel Books, 1991.

Bursik, Rose. *Amelia's Fantastic Flight*. New York: Henry Holt, 1992.

Calhoun, Mary. *Hot-Air Henry*. New York: Mulberry Books, 1981.

Gibbons, Gail. *Flying*. New York: Holiday House, 1985.

Greenstein, Elaine. *Emily and the Crows*. Saxonville, MA: Picture Book Studio, 1991.

Hoopes, Lyn Littlefield. *Wing-A-Ding*. Boston: Little, Brown, 1990.

Howe, James. *I Wish I Were a Butterfly*. San Diego, CA: Gulliver Books, 1987.

Jeunesse, Gallimard. *Airplanes and Flying Machines*. New York: Scholastic, 1989.

Lepscky, Ibi. *Leonardo da Vinci*. New York: Barron's, 1984.

From *Holiday Story Play*, copyright 1993. Libraries Unlimited/Teacher Ideas Press, P.O. Box 6633, Englewood, CO 80155-6633.

Nerlove, Miriam. *If All the World Were Paper*. Morton Grove, IL: Albert Whitman, 1991.

Provensen, Alice, and Martin Provensen. *The Glorious Flight: Across the Channel with Louis Bleriot*. New York: Puffin Books, 1983.

_____. *Leonardo da Vinci*. Viking Press, 1984.

Rockwell, Anne. *Planes*. New York: E. P. Dutton, 1985.

Taylor, Barbara. *Up, Up and Away: The Science of Flight*. New York: Random House, 1991.

Testa, Fulvio. *The Paper Airplane*. Faellanden, Switzerland: North-South Books, 1981.

Tibo, Gilles. *Simon and the Wind*. Montreal: Tundra Books, 1989.

Tusa, Tricia. *Maebelle's Suitcase*. New York: Aladdin Books, 1987.

Yolen, Jane. *Wings*. San Diego, CA: Harcourt Brace Jovanovich, 1991.

Woodruff, Elvira. *The Wing Shop*. New York: Holiday House, 1991.

Reference Book

Wiswell, Phil. *Kids' Games*. New York: Doubleday, 1987.

Music

Copus, Pamela, and Joyce Harlow. "Wings." *Holiday Story Play Music*. Plano, TX: Dreamtime Productions, P.O. Box 940061, Plano, TX 75094-0061.

ABOUT THE AUTHORS

Joyce Harlow has taught kindergarten through the fifth grade. She presently teaches kindergarten at Summerfield Academy in Spring, Texas. In addition to being a validator for N.A.E.Y.C., she conducts workshops and teacher in-service training based on the concepts from her books, *Story Play* and *Holiday Story Play*.

Victoria Saibara has taught prekindergarten, kindergarten, and first grade in the Houston, Texas, area for nine years. She conducts teacher training workshops based on *Holiday Story Play*. Victoria is the daughter of Joyce Harlow.

9 781563 081156